PALLADIO IN AMERICA

Rizzoli NEW YORK / electa editrice

Prepared and produced by Electa Editrice, Milano

Published in the United States of America
in 1978 by

Rizzoli INTERNATIONAL PUBLICATIONS, INC.
712 Fifth Avenue/New York 10019

© 1976 in Italy by Electa Editrice, Milano

Library of Congress Catalog Card Number: 77-95342
ISBN: 0-8478-0169-1

Printed in Italy by Fantonigrafica - Venice

PALLADIO IN AMERICA

The Work of Andrea Palladio as represented in an
exhibition sent to the United States in 1976 by the
Centro Internazionale di Studi di Architettura
Andrea Palladio of Vicenza,
with the assistance of the Government of Italy

by Walter Muir Whitehill

with an essay on Palladio's influence
on American architecture

by Frederick Doveton Nichols

FOREWORD

The Centro di Architettura "Andrea Palladio" of Vicenza, organizer of the "Mostra del Palladio" held in the Basilica in Vicenza in 1973, is particurlarly happy and honoured to have been entrusted by the Government of Italy to be the bearer of a cultural message that this Country is sending to the United States to celebrate the Bicentennial of the American Independence.

"Palladio in America", by presenting to the American public architectural ideals that tie the two Countries together, acknowledges the important part Palladio had in the development of an architectural culture which took place in, and is a testimony of those historical events that shaped the national unity of the United States and had in Thomas Jefferson its most prestigious exponent.

The Centro is most indebted to Professors Walter M. Whitehill and Frederick D. Nichols, co-authors of the catalogue, who tirelessly organized the exhibit in the United States and to whom we express our deepest appreciation. We also thank the Board of Visitors of the University of Virginia; the Directors of the Corcoran Gallery of Art in Washington, the Museum of Fine Arts in Boston and the National Park Service for the Second United States Bank in Philadelphia, who, through their kindness, made available to the Centro their galleries; to the Cultural Institutions in the United States which will give hospitality to the exhibition while in the Country. And foremost we extend our deep gratitude to all our Friends in the United States who, in their own capacity, helped to make "Palladio in America" a reality.

Finally, the Centro wishes to express its thanks to the "Compagnia di Navigazione Italia" for the kind help given in the shipping of the material of the Palladio exhibitions from Italy to the United States.

Guglielmo Cappelletti
President
*Centro Internazionale di Architettura
"Andrea Palladio"*

INTRODUCTION

In July 1972 I visited Vicenza for the first time. I had gone with no more serious purpose that spending a few days between a wedding in Switzerland and a visit in Florence. It proved a happy accident, however; for Frederick Doveton Nichols, Cary D. Langhorne Professor of Architecture at the University of Virginia, thoughtfully told two of his friends of my presence. In consequence, through the extraordinary kindness of Dr. Vittor Luigi Braga Rosa and Commendatore Hereward Watlington, my wife and I were introduced to the world of Andrea Palladio under the most sympathetic circumstances. On the first morning we were taken to the Villa Rotonda, and for the remainder of the day through the countryside, visiting villa after villa. On the following days we were shown the monuments of Vicenza. It delighted me that in the Palazzo Valmarana-Braga, rescued and restored by Dr. Braga Rosa after wartime damage, was installed the Centro Internazionale di Studi di Architettura Andrea Palladio. This group of architectural historians maintained a library and photograph collection centered upon the work of Palladio, sponsored annual international conferences, and were engaged in publishing a Corpus Palladianum *of profusely illustrated folio monographs on Palladio's principal buildings, with editions both in Italian and English.*

It was a rare treat to explore a wholly unfamiliar region, and to find in the Centro all the scholarly resources that explained the local monuments. Moreover, we found that in preparation for a great exhibition to be held the following year, the Centro had commissioned the construction by Pietro Ballico of Schio of a series of wooden models of a number of Palladio's buildings. As these were to a common scale (1:33), they conveyed a better sense of relative magnitude than could be obtained from photographs. We were taken to the disused church of San Silvestro in Vicenza where a number of the completed models were stored in anticipation of the 1973 exhibition. In the course of this visit I lost my heart to Vicenza and the Veneto and was happy to have gained the friendship of some of its residents who were devoted to architectural history and historic preservation.

Later in July 1972, when Dr. Braga came to England to visit buildings of Palladian derivation, I took him to lunch at Boodle's in St. James's Street, built in 1775, so that he might see the interior of the first floor Saloon, with its huge Palladian window. Early in January 1973, when he had come to the United States to see Mr. Jefferson's University of Virginia, he came to North Andover, Massachusetts, to spend a night with us. During this brief visit, when New England snow and ice contrasted unfavorably with the Veneto, we conceived the idea that the catalogue of the Centro's 1973 exhibition might contain an English summary that I would prepare. Consequently late in

March 1973, after a month that we had spent in Rome following my retirement from the directorship of the Boston Athenaeum, we returned to the Veneto to spend a week with Dr. Braga at his Villa Rosa at Tramonte (Padova). We visited more Palladian buildings in Vicenza, Venice, and the countryside, but as the exhibition catalogue was not yet completed the project of making it bi-lingual fell by the wayside.

Vicenza celebrated 1973 as an Anno Palladiano. The great Mostra del Palladio, which filled the Basilica from 30 May to 4 November, contained the series of scale models, fine photographs, original drawings lent by the Royal Institute of British Architects and other owners, paintings, and the numerous editions of the printed works of Palladio. It was divided into sections explaining the relation of Palladio not only to the ancient world but his Renaissance contemporaries, his work, his subsequent influence upon architects in many countries, and his writings, together with the literature of Palladianism. It was a magnificent tribute, superbly installed, in the ideal setting. The director of the exhibition was Renato Cevese, professor of architectural history at the University of Padova and secretary of the Centro. A detailed scholarly catalogue entitled Mostra del Palladio, Vicenza / Basilica Palladiana *was published by Electa Editrice in Milano; the text represented an international collaboration between Professor Cevese and Professors Erik Forssman, Wolfgang Lotz, Peter Murray, Howard Burns, Lionello Puppi, and Rodolfo Pallucchini.*

When we returned to Vicenza late in August 1973 to see the Mostra, Professor Nichols with a number of architectural students from the University of Virginia was installed in the guest house of the Villa Foscari (La Malcontenta), just outside Venice. We joined them in visits to various villas in the company of Dr. Braga, who proved the ideal guide. The enthusiasm aroused by the Mostra was such that the Centro had decided to continue it in Vicenza during the summer of 1974; there were already numerous requests that it might travel abroad. Professor Nichols and I were anxious that at least part of it might be shown at the University of Virginia. Consequently before leaving Vicenza we had a discussion with Professor Cevese and with On. Avv. Guglielmo Cappelletti, President of the Centro, about that possibility.

In the course of 1975 the Palladio exhibition travelled to a number of European cities. For its appearance in Vienna, Martin Kubelik prepared an Austrian catalogue. In London, where it was shown under the auspices of the Arts Council of Great Britain and the Centro, the models were augmented by many distinguished additions from British collections. There the emphasis was on Palladio himself, without reference to his great contributions to British architecture. The London catalogue,

Andrea Palladio 1508-1580, The portico and the farmyard, *was by Howard Burns in collaboration with Lynda Fairbairn and Bruce Boucher; it is an admirable book that can be used with pleasure for its own sake.*

On 13 April 1976, the 233rd birthday of Thomas Jefferson, the University of Virginia will dedicate the Rotunda that he designed as the crown of his "academical village". In its original form, Mr. Jefferson had created three oval rooms on the ground and the first floors. On the upper floor there was, in his words, "a single room for a Library, canopied by the Dome and it's sky-light". His inspiration came from the Pantheon, which he knew only through the prints of Piranesi and the writings of Palladio. Indeed Giacomo Leoni's 1721 edition of Palladio was Mr. Jefferson's principal source of information for the design of the building, even to its name, for Palladio refers to "the Pantheon, at present call'd the Rotunda". A fire in 1895 destroyed the interior of Mr. Jefferson's Rotunda, leaving little of the original fabric except the exterior walls. During the subsequent reconstruction, Stanford White completely altered the plan, converting the first and upper stories into one vast library, with a gigantic colonnade of single columns supporting balconied book stacks. When the library moved elsewhere more than forty years ago, the purpose of White's design evaporated; there remained only a vast empty apartment, useful for nothing in particular. After several decades of this desolation, the University of Virginia recently found the means to restore the Rotunda's interior to the form designed by Mr. Jefferson.

Even before the workmen had completed their tasks, it was evident that the great upper room, surrounded by two balconies supported by a range of paired columns, and covered by the dome, was the most dramatic enclosure of space achieved by an American architect during the Roman phase of the classical revival. When this room is dedicated, restored to its original form, derived from Rome by way of Palladio, it will happily contain for the occasion ten of the Palladio models from Vicenza. In commemoration of the Bicentennial of the American Revolution, the Government of Italy has assisted the Centro Internazionale di Studi di Architettura Andrea Palladio to send a part of the 1973 Vicenza Mostra to the United States during 1976. It is singularly appropriate that the exhibition should open in a Palladian building designed by the author of the Declaration of Independence. After some weeks at the University of Virginia, the exhibition will travel north to Washington, Philadelphia, Boston, and several other cities before returning to Italy, possibly by way of Japan.

When the Centro wished to have a publication in English prepared for this American tour, I indiscreetly volunteered to do it. My motives for writing upon a subject in which I have no

scholarly competence are simple. I have devoted many years to architectural history of earlier and later periods: to Romanesque Spain of the eleventh century and to my native Boston from its settlement in 1630 to the present. As I only came to know and love Palladio's buildings a very few years ago, I hope that I may be able to lead some of my compatriots along a similar road by means of the pages that follow. It is sometimes easier to convey the results of a recent enthusiasm, from a small store of lately acquired information, than to transform into simple terms the product of long years of research. This is, then, simply a picture book with brief text, designed to introduce American visitors to the exhibition to the work of Andrea Palladio and to provide them with something that they may wish to keep afterward as a reminder of the exhibition.

Wherever possible, I have described buildings by quoting Andrea Palladio's comments from the 1738 English translation by Isaac Ware, published in London as The Four Books of Andrea Palladio's Architecture. *A facsimile of this book, with excellent reproductions of the plates was published in 1965 by Dover Publications, Inc. of New York, with a new introduction by Adolf K. Placzek of the Avery Library, Columbia University. Fortunately it is still available at a remarkably reasonable price. In quoting, I have followed exactly Ware's text, even when his punctuation and liberal use of apostrophes differ from current usage.*

The eleven buildings that are represented by scale models are described in greater detail than those that appear only in photographic reproduction. What I say about them, and indeed almost everything in this book, is derived from the Centro's 1973 catalogue of the Vicenza Mostra, from volumes of its Corpus Palladianum, *from Professor Lionello Puppi's* Andrea Palladio *(Milano: Electa Editrice, 1973), Professor James S. Ackerman's* Palladio *(Penguin Books, 1966), from Martin Kubelik's Vienna and Howard Burns's London exhibition catalogues, both of 1975. Although I have seen the greater part of Palladio's buildings, I have done no research in original documents; everything that I have to say is derived from one or more of the scholars mentioned above.*

The account of Goethe's passage through the Veneto in 1786 is drawn from the admirable translation of his Italienische Reise *by the late W. H. Auden and Elisabeth Mayer, published in 1962 by Pantheon Books as* Italian Journey (1786-1788). *His comments are memorable in showing how much alive the spirit of Palladio was more than two centuries after the death of his body. Close to another two centuries later, I found the situation unchanged.*

Professor Frederick D. Nichols has contributed an independent essay upon Palladio's influence upon American architec-

ture, which at the time of writing I have not seen. I call the particular attention of American readers to his article, "The Villas of Andrea Palladio, 1508-1580" in the August 1973 issue of the magazine Antiques, for the color photographs by Joseph C. Farber that illustrate it give a singularly vivid impression of some of Palladio's buildings.

Professor Nichols and his colleague at the University of Virginia, Mario di Valmarana, have been exceedingly helpful to me throughout this undertaking. I have enjoyed a conversation with Douglas Lewis, Curator of Sculpture at the National Gallery of Art, Washington, D.C., who has given me copies of some of his articles on Palladian themes.

The Centro in Vicenza has undertaken to provide the illustrations that I have requested. I am grateful to them for this kindness, and to Dr. Massimo Vitta Zelman and his colleagues at Electa Editrice who have made themselves responsible for the design and production of this book in an incredibly short time.

I am grateful to all of them, and to Dr. Braga Rosa and Professor Cevese and their Vicenza friends and colleagues of the Centro for having allowed me to have a share in introducing the exhibition to the United States.

Walter Muir Whitehill

North Andover, Massachusetts
19 December 1975

ANDREAS PALLADIVS VICENTINVS.

A few hours after he arrived in Vicenza on 19 September 1786 Johann Wolfgang von Goethe had already visited the Teatro Olimpico and other buildings by Palladio, concluding: "You have to see these buildings with your own eyes to realize how good they are. No reproductions of Palladio's designs give an adequate idea of the harmony of their dimensions; they must be seen in their actual perspective." This was early in the second week of Goethe's first sight of Italy; an enterprise lasting a year and a half that he began soon after his thirty-seventh birthday. Two days later he called on the architect O. Bertotti Scamozzi, whose four volume work, *Le Fabbriche e i Disegni di Andrea Palladio* had been published in Venice between 1776 and 1783. The same afternoon Goethe visited the Villa Rotonda, of which he wrote: "Architecture has never, perhaps, achieved a greater degree of luxury". On the 22nd he attended a meeting of the Accademia Olimpica in a large hall next door to the Teatro Olimpico. Palladio's name kept cropping up in the discussion; to Goethe "it was gratifying to see that, even after such a long time, Palladio is still revered by his fellow citizens as a lodestar and an example".

In Padua on the 27th he noted in his journal: "At last I have acquired the works of Palladio, not the original edition with woodcuts, but a facsimile with copperplate engravings, published by Smith, an excellent man who was formerly English consul in Venice. One must give the English credit for having so long appreciated what is good and for their munificence and remarkable skill in publicizing it". He remarked on the sociable nature of Italian bookshops. "There were half a dozen people there when I entered, and when I asked for the works of Palladio, they all focused their attention on me. While the proprietor was looking for the book, they spoke highly of it and gave me all kinds of information about the original edition and the reprint. They were well acquainted both with the work and with the merits of the author. Taking me for an architect, they complimented me on my desire to study this master who had more useful and practical suggestions to offer than even Vitruvius, since he had made a thorough study of classical antiquity and tried to adapt his knowledge to the needs of our times". Note, in passing, that although Palladio had been in his grave for two hundred and six years both Goethe and the citizens of Padua felt that he was still meeting "the needs of our times".

After visiting the Convento della Carità and Il Redentore in Venice, Goethe became even more absorbed in Palladio, "a great man who does not wish to conform to the world but to transform it in accordance with his own high ideals". After the passage of some days, he wrote: "Looking at the buildings which Palladio completed, in particular at his churches, I have found much to criticize side by side with great excellence. While I was asking myself how far I was right or wrong about this extraordinary man, he seemed to be standing by me, saying: 'This or that I did against my will, nevertheless I did it because it was the closest approximation to my ideal possible under the circumstances'. The more I think about him, the more strongly I feel that, when he looked at the height and width of an old church or house for which he had to make a new façade, he must have said to himself: 'How can you give this building the noblest form possible? Because of contradictory demands, you are bound to bungle things here and there, and it may well happen that there will be some incongruities. But the building as a whole will be in a noble style, and you will enjoy doing the work'. It was in this way that he executed the great conception he had in mind, even when it was not quite suitable and he had to mangle it in the details".

During a walk on the Lido, Goethe stumbled upon the English cemetery, where Joseph Smith (1682-1779), "the good consul", was buried. "To him I owe my copy of Palladio, and I offered up a grateful prayer at his unconsecrated grave, which was half buried in the sand".

When Marta, the lame wife of Pietro della Gondola, a hatmaker (later to be a miller) gave birth to a son in Padua on 30 November 1508, the infant was named Andrea, in honor of the saint on whose festival he was born. Not even the most imaginative gypsy would have dared to predict that that child would be remembered centuries thence, and be greatly admired by one of the outstanding minds of European civilization. Nothing in heredity or environment would have given ground for such an unlikely suggestion. Indeed Andrea di Pietro, as he was known for the first thirty-odd years of his life, was no infant prodigy. At the age of thirteen he was apprenticed to Bartolomeo Cavazza, a stonemason in Padua, for a period of six years, a term that he did not serve, for he was taken to Vicenza by his father in 1523. The following year he was enrolled in the guild of stonemasons of Vicenza as an apprentice of Giovanni de Pedemuro and Girolamo Pittoni, the best carvers of architectural sculpture in the city. After he had completed his apprenticeship, Andrea di Pietro continued to work

1. Portrait of Palladio engraved by Picart.

for and live in the house of Giovanni de Pedemuro until 1534 when he married a servant girl with the pleasing name of Allegradonna, by whom he eventually had at least four sons and a daughter.

Although a small city, Vicenza was a rich and cultivated one. Its neighbors Padua, Brescia, and Verona were far larger; at a time when Vicenza had some twenty thousand inhabitants, Venice had perhaps one hundred and fifty thousand. Vicenza having come under the domination of Venice in 1404, the principal officers of government were two Venetian nobles, the *Podestà* and the *Capitanio*, who served a sixteen-month term of office. Although these officials received instructions in matters of policy directly from Venice, the nobility of Vicenza shared in the daily administration of the city. A Great Council, composed of all adult male nobles, annually elected from their number a Council of One Hundred, which would choose eight Deputies, who served two month terms. It was thus a city without a hereditary court, in which a local rotating oligarchy wielded considerable power even though ultimate authority rested in Venice.

The nobles of Vicenza were a remarkably educated and industrious lot. It has been noted that often more than forty of the members of the Council of One Hundred would be the holders of doctorates, usually in law, of the University of Padua. The land of the province had remained in local hands and was farmed to good purpose; whereas Venetians had bought up much of the land in the provinces of Padua and Treviso, they had hardly an agricultural toe-hold in Vicenza. Thus the city was rich not only from the cultivation of grain, fruit, wine, and cattle, but from a thriving silk industry, which exported goods to the trade fairs of France and Germany. It was a place where wealth, leisure, and education were widely enough diffused to develop a sense of community pride and ambition, and to provide fertile ground for new ideas.

Count Giangiorgio Trissino (1478-1550), who had been in the service of Popes Leo X and Clement VIII, and who knew not only princes but the leading literary and artistic figures throughout Italy, determined in his mid-fifties to build a new loggia in the classical style of the Roman Renaissance at his villa at Cricoli, on the outskirts of Vicenza. Andrea di Pietro had the good fortune to be hired for some of the masonry and carving on this new structure, which was the first instance of Renaissance building in Vicenza. Trissino, a poet, dramatist, philologist, and antiquarian, planned to create an informal humanistic academy at his villa by inviting a group of young nobles to join his household as resident students. His enthusiasm for architecture caused him to follow the work on his villa with close attention; thus he came to know Andrea, and, finding him promising, decided to educate him with the young nobles.

As Andrea was in his mid-twenties when he came into this surprising scene, and can have had next to no previous formal education, time was too short for him to become a well-rounded Humanist in the Renaissance ideal of the universal man. But Trissino set him to studying everything that pertained to the architecture, engineering, topography, and military science of the world of ancient Rome. Trissino's object was to make possible the architectural adornment of Vicenza; to this end he gave Andrea the training of an expert. Having turned a stonemason into an incipient architect and scholar, Trissino proceeded in 1540 to give his new man the new name of Palladio. It was an elegantly oblique reference to the wisdom of Pallas Athena, as well as the Italian form of the name of the Roman writer of the fourth century, Rutilius Taurus Aemilianus Palladius, whose works dealt with the farming life of country villas. By this metamorphosis the stonemason Andrea di Pietro became the architect Andrea Palladio.

Trissino enlarged his protegé's horizons by travel. Thrice he took Palladio with him to Rome so that he might study those monuments of Roman architecture that had remained standing. Through Trissino Palladio met the principal architects of his time. Above all this connection brought commissions for villas and palaces in Vicenza. Palladio began to build the Villa Godi at Lonedo di Lugo and the Palazzo Civena in Vicenza before his first trip to Rome in 1541 with Trissino. The year after his return came the commission for the great Palazzo Thiene in Vicenza.

For decades Vicenza had been wrestling with the problem of replacing the loggias around the fifteenth-century Basilica — the most conspicuous building in the city — which had begun to collapse in 1496. More than a third of a century passed with the Piazza dei Signori in a mess. Between 1538 and 1542 Jacopo Sansovino, Sebastiano Serlio, Michele Sanmicheli, and Giulio Romano were consulted, without a solution being achieved. Andrea Palladio presented a design in 1546, which was finally adopted in 1549. It is not improbable that Palladio's trips to Rome with Trissino in 1545 and again in 1546-47 were intended, at least in part, to prepare him for this supremely important commission.

Once Andrea Palladio was accepted as the architect for the renovation of the Basilica, he was clearly established as the man who should be employed by right-thinking Vicentines for their own houses. For three decades following his rebirth in 1540 Palladio designed villas for Vicentines and Venetians in various parts of the Veneto. The commissions that he received beyond the boundaries of the province of Vicenza sprang from a new desire of the sixteenth century nobility of Venice to make better use of the lands that some of them owned on the adjacent *terra firma*, or mainland. As a maritime power, Venice had long looked only to the sea. Nevertheless it was vulnerable to attack from the land, and its grain and other food supplies had to be imported. Expansion on the mainland in the direction of Treviso and Padua would safeguard the flanks of Venice and provide nearby sources of provisions. Moreover by draining swamps, building canals, reclaiming land, and by introducing improved practices of agriculture, large scale farming could become a profitable form of investment, free from the risks of maritime trade. Such enterprises, however, if they were to be fully successful, required personal oversight by the owners. So in the second and third quarters of the sixteenth century there came to be an increasing number of Venetian gentlemen, living upon their land, who called upon Palladio for the design of their villas.

From 1540 until his death in 1580 Palladio also built palaces and public buildings, almost entirely in Vicenza, the face of which he substantially changed. Only in the last two decades of his life was he conspicuously employed in Venice, and there upon churches and monastic buildings, which he had not designed in earlier life. The record of his accomplishment will be seen in the descriptions of specific buildings that form the next sections of this catalogue.

Palladio was fortunate throughout his life in having patrons who encouraged his studies of classical antiquity, put him in the way of receiving commissions for buildings, and introduced him to scenes that would ordinarily have been closed to one of his humble origins. Although Count Giangiorgio Trissino died in 1550, Palladio during the remainder of his life enjoyed the patronage and friendship of the noble Venetian humanist brothers, Daniele and Marc' Antonio Barbaro, both of whom were connoiseurs of architecture. Daniele, who studied at the University of Padua from 1537 to 1545, where he created

a botanic garden, went abroad in 1549-1551 as Venetian ambassador to England and Scotland. While there he was nominated as successor to Giovanni Grimani, Patriarch of Aquileia. Although that designation carried with it no current ecclesiastical duties, it debarred him from government service. So Daniele Barbaro devoted his talents to humanistic studies and to the family estate at Maser (Treviso), from which most of his income was derived. For that property Palladio designed a magnificent villa that will be described in a later chapter. The management of that property indeed became Daniele Barbaro's lifetime occupation, for he died in 1570 before Grimani, whom he was designated to succeed in the patriarchate.

Marc' Antonio Barbaro had an active career in the service of the state, including embassies to Paris and Constantinople, that in no way diminished his interest in architecture; during the last quarter of the sixteenth century he had some hand in most of the public building projects in Venice. These brothers were as distinguished and knowledgeable patrons as an architect could have. The enduring quality of the friendship is indicated by an inscription over the portal of the Tempietto of Maser that Palladio designed in the last year of his life for Marc' Antonio Barbaro where the names of the patron and the architect are recorded with equal billing.

On Palladio's last trip to Rome in 1554 he accompanied Daniele Barbaro and other gentlemen from Venice. This journey led to Palladio's first publication, *L'antichità di Roma*, a guide book to the city, drawn from his own observations and from ancient and contemporary writings. It was first published during his stay in Rome, but was also issued at Venice in 1554. It went through various editions and translations, appearing in French at Arras in 1612 and in a Latin version at Rome in 1618-1619. Daniele Barbaro at the same time was engaged in translating and preparing a commentary upon the architectural treatise of Vitruvius Pollio, the Roman architect and engineer of the era of Augustus. Palladio provided the illustrations for *I dieci libri dell'architettura di M. Vitruvio tradutti et commentati da mons. Barbaro patriarca eletto di Aquileggia*, published at Venice in 1556. Palladio thus had a double road to knowledge of Roman architecture. Through collaboration with Barbaro he was familiar with ancient texts; through his own travels and observations he was able to study the extant monuments. He sketched and measured buildings, not to attain an artistic remembrance of a picturesque site, as Piranesi did

2. Quattro Libri. *Title page of the first edition, 1570.*

3. Quattro Libri. *Title page of the Ware translation, 1738.*

later, but to carry away a geometric rendering for future possible use in his own work.

For most of his life Palladio was poor. He was fifty years old before he reached even the lowest rank that was subject to taxation, yet his abilities and, one suspects, his personal charm, gained him ready acceptance in the highest circles. When the Accademia Olimpica was organized in Vicenza in 1556 for the promotion of the arts and sciences, especially of mathematics, he was a member, although the other twenty-one founders were nobles, scholars, or mathematicians. When the academy ventured into theatrical productions as a means of showing publicly the cultivation of Vicenza, Palladio took an active part. For the performance of Trissino's *Sofonisba* in 1562 in the Basilica, Palladio designed a demountable theatre, whose sets could be stored when not in use. When the project for a permanent one evolved in 1580, Palladio designed the Teatro Olimpico that was his last contribution to the adornment of Vicenza.

During the later years of his life, Palladio's finances somewhat improved. Although he was never well off, he was able to provide a 400 ducat dowry for his daughter Zenobia during the 1560s. His son Orazio was graduated as a doctor of laws at Padua in 1569; with his brothers Leonida and Silla, Orazio helped his father with correspondence and with the preparation of the treatise on architecture on which he was engaged. Another son, Marc' Antonio, was a sculptor and a skilful draughtsman.

The thought of writing a treatise on architecture probably went back to Palladio's early years with Trissino. It was a good third of a century in ripening, as Palladio simultaneously increased his own knowledge of the ancient world and his experience in building villas and palaces. It was more substantial than a dream, for Daniele Barbaro in 1556 and 1568 referred to a manuscript. *I Quattro Libri di Architettura* was published at Venice in 1570 by Dominico de' Franceschi. The work was a blending of his studies of classical architecture with his own experience in contemporary design and construction. The first book dealt with materials, the orders, and decorative ornaments; the second with domestic architecture illustrated by his own villas and palaces and by his reconstructions of the dwellings of classical antiquity. The third book was concerned with ancient public buildings and town planning, bridges, and basilicas, and the fourth with Palladio's reconstruction of Roman temples, with a very few observations on their relation to Christian churches. When the *Quattro Libri* appeared, Palladio's experience as a designer of churches was still ahead of him.

The influence of this book upon the architecture of many countries over many centuries is immeasureable. It was reprinted at Venice in 1601, 1616, 1642, and 1711; it was the Venetian facsimile of 1768 that Goethe bought in Padua and took home with him to Weimar. Spanish translations appeared at Valladolid in 1625 and Madrid in 1797; French ones in 1650 and 1682. Although Inigo Jones carried home a copy of the *Quattro Libri* from his Italian tour of 1613-1614 and introduced the architecture of Palladio to England, it was 1721 before an English translation appeared in London, thanks to the enterprise of the Venetian Giacomo Leoni. As that version left something to be desired, Lord Burlington inspired a new translation by the architect Isaac Ware, that appeared in 1738. The bibliography of Palladio continues to grow even in our times; witness, the first translation into Polish, published in Warsaw in 1955!

From his years with Trissino, Palladio had maintained an interest in Roman military tactics, which he transmitted to his sons Leonida and Orazio, who made drawings illustrative of Caesar's *Commentaries*. When the sons died early in 1572, Palladio instigated the publication of an Italian edition of Caesar containing their drawings. *I Commentari di Giulio Cesare*, published at Venice in 1575 by Pietro de' Franceschi, contained a familiar Italian translation of the text; it was notable rather for its illustrations, and for the preface by Andrea Palladio, in which he explained his desire "to achieve some honoured memory for the name of my sons". This was the last book in which Palladio had a hand.

Palladio died in Vicenza in August 1580 in his seventy-second year. His personal appearance is as poorly documented as his architectural work is richly. There is no authentic contemporary likeness, though two eighteenth century engravings of very different appearance have wide currency. Leoni's 1721 London edition contains the likeness of a vigorous, clean-shaven man, who looks as if he were about to go to a building site and climb a ladder. This engraving by B. Picart was reputed to come from a painting by Paolo Veronese. F. Muttoni's *Architettura di Andrea Palladio*, published at Venice in 1740-1748, contains a portrait engraved by Francesco Zucchi after Giovanni Battista Mariotti of a grave, bearded older man wearing an approximation of a cassock, who seems more on the point of praying than overseeing construction. This was reputed to have been engraved from a portrait owned at the time by the Capra family (of the

I COMMENTARI
DI C. GIVLIO
CESARE,

CON LE FIGVRE IN RAME DE GLI
alloggiamenti, de' fatti d'arme, delle circonuallationi delle cit-
tà, & di molte altre cose notabili descritte in essi.

Fatte da ANDREA PALLADIO per facilitare
a chi legge, la cognition dell'historia.

CON PRIVILEGI.

IN VENETIA,

APPRESSO PIETRO DE FRANCESCHI.
M. D. LXXV.

4. Title page of Cesar's Commentaries.

Villa Rotonda) that cannot today be located. Even if it could, it would still not be a contemporary likeness, for its painter, Mariotti, was born several years after Palladio's death. As these are all there are, both likenesses are reproduced here.

Although the men appear to be quite different, I recall the dissimilarities between two portraits of the Boston silversmith Paul Revere (1735-1818). John Singleton Copley painted Revere at the age of 35, working in his shirtsleeves at his bench, with a silver teapot in hand. Gilbert Stuart painted him in his upper seventies, with his coat on, seated in the dignified manner of a man who had graduated from working with his hands to be an industrial entrepreneur. There is as much, or as little, difference between the two posthumous likenesses of Palladio as there is between the two life portraits of Revere. Although the Picart engraving is often described as a fantasy, Professor Ackerman chose to reproduce it on the back cover of his book on Palladio; I suspect because the more vigorous portrait corresponds more closely to our vision of what Palladio ought to have looked like.

Andrea Palladio began the second of his four books on architecture with a chapter concerning the decorum or conveniency that ought to be observed in private fabrics. Having dealt with this principle he proceeded in the second chapter to a discussion of the disposition of rooms, which is so characteristic and fundamental that it deserves quotation (in the eighteenth century English of Isaac Ware), for he is concerned that decorum extend even to the most utilitarian parts of a building.

"That the houses may be commodious for the use of the family ... great care ought to be taken, not only in the principal parts, as the loggia, halls, court, magnificent rooms, and ample stairs, light and easy of ascent; but also, that the most minute and least beautiful parts be accommodated to the service of the greatest and more worthy: for as in the human body there are some noble and beautiful parts, and some rather ignoble and disagreeable, and yet we see that those stand in very great need of these, and without them they could not subsist; so in fabricks, there ought to be some parts considerable and honoured, and some less elegant; without which the other cou'd not remain free, and so consequently wou'd lose part of their dignity and beauty. But as our Blessed Creator has ordered these our members in such a manner, that the most beautiful are in places most exposed to view, and the less comely more hidden; so in building also, we ought to put the principal and considerable parts, in places the most seen, and the less beautiful, in places as much hidden from the eye as possible; that in them may be lodged all the foulness of the house, and all those things that may give any obstruction, and in any measure render the more beautiful parts disagreeable. I approve therefore that in the lowest part of the fabric, which I make somewhat underground, may be disposed the cellars, the magazines for wood, pantries, kitchens, servants-halls, wash-houses, and such like things necessary for daily use. From which disposition follow two conveniencies, the one that the upper part remains all free; and the other and no less important, is, that the said upper apartments are wholesomer to live in, the floor being at a distance from the damps of the ground; besides as it rises, it is more agreeable to be looked at, and to look out of. It is also to be observed, that in the remaining part of the fabric there may be great, middle-sized, and small rooms, and all near one another, that they may be reciprocally made use of".

The third chapter, concerned with the design of townhouses, opens thus: "I am convinced, that in the opinion of those, who shall see the following fabrics, and know how difficult it is to introduce a new custom, especially in building, of which profession everyone is persuaded that he knows his part, I shall be esteemed very fortunate, to have found gentlemen of so noble and generous a disposition, and of such excellent judgment, as to have hearkened to my reasons, and departed from that antiquated custom of building without grace or any beauty at all; and, indeed, I cannot but very heartily thank God, as we ought in all our actions to do, for granting me such a share of his favour, as to have been able to put into practice many of those things, which I have learnt from my very great fatigues and voyages, and by my great study. And altho' some of the designed fabrics are not entirely finished, yet may one by what is done comprehend what the whole will be when finished. I have prefixed to each the name of the builder, and the place where they are, that every one may, if he pleases, really see how they succeed. And here the reader may take notice, that in placing the said designs, I have had respect neither to the rank or dignity of the gentlemen to be mentioned; but I have inserted them where I thought most convenient: not but they are all very honourable".

After dealing with palaces in towns, Palladio proceeds in chapter thirteen to discuss "the elegant and convenient disposition" of a villa, once an "agreeable, pleasant, com-

5. Portrait of Palladio engraved by Zucchi.

19

modious, and healthy situation" has been chosen. The noble owners required handsome lodging for themselves that they considered suitable to their station in the world, as well as accommodation for their servants, animals, and farm equipment. For the convenient blending of these needs, Palladio's principle of decorum offered a happy solution. A Palladian villa in the Veneto was something new in country life. It was not a stronghold, as it would have been earlier; it was not a simple farmhouse of utilitarian inelegance, nor was it an elegant country retreat near a city, designed purely for rest and amusement. It was definitely in the country, often at a considerable distance from a city. While it was what was thought of later in England as "a gentleman's country seat", it was also the headquarters of a working farm that produced income. So Palladio indicated that "there are two sorts of fabricks required in a villa: one is for the habitation of the master, and of his family; and the other to manage and take care of the produce and animals of the villa. Therefore the compartment of the site ought to be in such manner, that the one may not be any impediment to the other".

"The habitation for the master ought to be made with a just regard to his family and condition, and as has been observed in cities, of which mention has been made". The owner must not feel that he is in a wilderness, remote from the delights of civilization!

"The covertures for the things belonging to a villa, must be made suitable to the estate and number of animals; and in such manner joined to the master's habitation, that he may be able to go to every place under cover, that neither the rains, nor the scorching sun of the summer, may be a nuisance to him, when he goes to look after his affairs; which will also be of great use to lay wood in under cover, and an infinite number of things belonging to a villa, that would otherwise be spoiled by the rains and the sun: besides which these portico's will be a great ornament". How thoroughly Thomas Jefferson took this paragraph to heart when he designed Monticello two centuries later!

"Regard must be had in lodging the men employ'd for the use of the villa, the animals, the products, and the instruments, conveniently, and without any constraint". Palladio deals in turn with stables, cellars, granaries, and store-rooms, concluding the chapter with this advice: "Hay-lofts ought to face the south or west, because the hay being dried by the heat of the sun, it will not be in danger of corrupting and taking fire. The instruments necessary to the husband-men, must be in convenient places under cover towards the south. The grange, where the corn is threshed, ought to be exposed to the sun, ample, spacious, paved, and a little raised in the middle, with portico's round it, or at least on one side; that in case of sudden rains, the corn may be immediately conveyed under cover; and must not be too near the master's house, by reason of the dust, nor so far off as to be out of sight".

Palladio's villas were not only designed functionally; they were also relatively economical in construction. They were mostly built of rough brick, covered with stucco. There was a minimum of carved stone details; often the columns were of stuccoed brick. Palladio seldom repeated himself in plan or elevation, although in all he followed his guiding principles of harmony and composition.

Among the models that have been sent to the United States for this exhibition there is one of the Palazzo Chiericati in Vicenza and six of the villas. The common scale employed in building these will permit the viewer to appreciate more readily the variety of Palladio's design and plans. These will now be described in sequence. There will follow descriptions of the public buildings, secular and ecclesiastical, of which there are models. Other works of Palladio that are represented in the exhibition only by photographs will be described more briefly in a final section.

PALLADIO'S BUILDINGS
represented by scale models

VILLA SARACENO
Finale di Agugliaro (Vicenza)

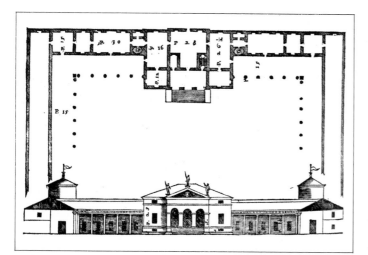

6. *Villa Saraceno, Finale di Agugliaro (Vicenza), from the* Quattro Libri, *II Book, p. 56, Venice, 1570.*

7. *Villa Saraceno, 1545, Finale di Agugliaro (Vicenza). Façade.*

In chapter fifteen of the second book, "Of the Designs of the Villa's belonging to some gentlemen of the Terra Firma", Palladio began with the following paragraph: "At a place in the Vicentine, called Finale, is the following building belonging to Signor Biagio Sarraceno. The floor of the rooms is raised five feet above the ground; the larger rooms are one square and five eighths in length, and in height equal to their breadth, and with flat cielings. The height also continues to the hall. The small rooms, near the loggia, are vaulted; the height of the vaults is equal to that of the rooms. The cellars are underneath, and the granaries above, which take up the whole body of the house. The kitchens are without the house, but so joined, that they are convenient. On each side there are all the necessary places for the use of a villa".

This modest villa is now thought to have been built about 1545. The Saraceno family, who hailed from Vicenza, had land in Finale di Agugliaro that was in 1525 divided between the brothers Biagio and Giacomo. Fifteen years later Biagio added further acreage to his share. As a 1546 tax return lists a residence at Finale among Biagio Saraceno's belongings, it is presumably this villa. The engraving published by Palladio in 1570 shows a carved pediment and three statues adorning the loggia of the central pavillion. Even without these, the structure has a simple monumental dignity. The plan of the owner's portion is of the simplest. A wide flight of steps leads up to three arches that give upon a barrel-vaulted loggia, from which one enters a T-shaped hall, on either side of which are two rooms, one large and one small. The plan called for dependencies with Doric loggias on either side of the house, turning at right angles to enclose three sides of a courtyard. It was never completed, for there is only one modest wing to the right of the house; nor were the dove-cotes (shown at the angles of the *barchesse*) built.

The Villa Saraceno is now a farmhouse, occupied by the Lombardi family. Although the staircase leading to the loggia has been unfortunately altered, and the whole place is a good deal the worse for wear, the paintings on the vault of the loggia testify to the villa's earlier status as a gentleman's residence. Not even peeling stucco can detract from the dignity of the façade.

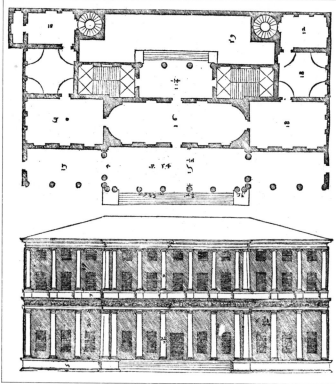

9. Palazzo Chiericati, 1550, Vicenza. Façade.
10. Palazzo Chiericati, Vicenza, from the Quattro Libri, *II Book, p. 6, Venice, 1570.*

The design of this palace, for which Palladio made plans in 1550, evolved naturally from the character of the site. Girolamo Chiericati wished to build upon a shallow lot with a wide frontage along one side of the open space, used as a cattle market and known as the Piazza dell'Isola, that extended to the river Bacchiglione. Palladio's plan called for a continuous loggia, running the length of the palace on the ground floor. As this would both improve the appearance of the square and provide shade and shelter for passers-by, Chiericati received permission in 1551 to extend the façade of his dwelling into the square over some thirteen feet of public ground. On the first floor, open loggias were provided only for three bays at the ends; between them at this level the main body of the house was extended over the central five bays of the ground floor loggia, thus providing a more spacious *salone* than the dimensions of Chiericati's site would have permitted.

Palladio thus described the palace: "This fabric has in the part below a loggia forwards, that takes in the whole front; the pavement of the first order rises above ground five foot; which has been done not only to put the cellars and other places underneath, that belong to the conveniency of the house, which wou'd not have succeeded if they had been made entirely under ground, because the river is not far from it; but also that the order above might the better enjoy the beautiful situation forwards. The larger have rooms the height of their vaults, according to the first method for the height of vaults: the middle-sized are with groined vaults, and their vaults are as high as those of the larger. The small rooms are also vaulted, and are divided off. All these vaults are adorned with most excellent compartments of stucco, by Messer Bartolomeo Ridolfi, a Veronese sculptor; and paintings by Messer Domenico Rizzo, and Messer Battista Venetiano, men singular in their profession. The hall is above in the middle of the front, and takes up the middle part of the loggia below. Its height is up to the roof; and because it projects forward a little, it has under the angles double columns. From one part to the other of this hall, there are two loggia's, that is on each side one; which have their soffites or ceilings adorned with very beautiful pictures, and afford a most agreeable sight. The first order of the front is Dorick, and the second Ionick".

The plan is symmetrical. The entrance in the center of the ground floor loggia leads to a room with semi-circular ends from which one proceeds, on either side, to

one large and two smaller rooms. The door opposite the entrance gives on a smaller loggia, which provides covered access to two staircases and gives upon a long and narrow courtyard, with a screen wall at the back of the property line. On the first floor the plan is similar, save that the central *salone* gains double the area of the entrance hall by extending over the five central bays of the ground floor loggia. From the first floor there are admirable views across the square to the river and the mills on the opposite bank.

The open space afforded by the Piazza dell'Isola permitted Palladio to design a façade that would have been inappropriate in an ordinary narrow city street. As it could be seen from a distance, the Palazzo Chiericati is more closely related to his villas than to his other palaces.

In 1554, when only the three bays on the left and part of the central block were completed, construction was interrupted; the building was finished only in the following century. The pinnacles and statues above the cornice are of this later period, and did not form part of Palladio's design. The Palazzo Chiericati now houses the Museo Civico of Vicenza.

VILLA PISANI
Montagnana (Padova)

The small fortified town of Montagnana is surrounded by modest walls with crenellations that remind one of ginger cookies. It suggests an operatic set or an illustration in a child's book of fairy stories rather than a fortress able to resist determined attack. Just outside the walls, near a town gate, is the villa that Palladio built about 1552 for a Venetian nobleman. In the fourteenth chapter of his second book, entitled "Of the Designs of the country-houses belonging to some noble Venetians", he thus described it: "The following fabrick is near the gate of Montagnana, a castle in the Padoano, and was built by the magnificent Signor Francesco Pisani; who being gone to a better life, could not finish it. The large rooms are one square and three quarters in length; the vaults are *à schisso*, and in height according to the second manner for the height of vaults. The middle sized are square, and vaulted *à cadino*. The small rooms, and the passage, are of an equal breadth: their vaults are two squares in height; the entrance has four columns, one fifth less than those without, which support the pavement of the hall, and make the height of the vaults beautiful, and secure. In the four niches that are seen there, have been carved the four seasons of the year, by Messer Alessandro Vittoria, an excellent sculptor. The first order of the columns is Dorick, the second Ionick. The rooms above, are with flat cielings. The height of the hall reaches up to the roof. This fabrick has two streets on the wings, where there are two doors; over which there are passages that lead to the kitchen, and places for servants".

Francesco Pisani's house is really a small palace rather than a typical villa, for it stands directly on a street outside the town walls, and has no farm buildings attached. Indeed Palladio's plan indicates an urban setting, for there appear as well to be streets on both sides of the central pavillion, spanned by modest triumphal arches, above which are enclosed passages that connect the wings only on the upper floor. Even if the magnificent Signor Pisani had not prematurely "gone to a better life", his house could hardly have been completed on this plan, for the site would not permit it. The left hand wing would have impinged upon the moat of the town wall.

Although the wings were never built, the central part of the house is handsome. The floor plan of the two stories is identical and completely symmetrical. The ground floor has the Doric order, with a continuous entablature, while the Ionic order is used for the upper story. Along the front the orders are represented by half columns, while on the back, where there are loggias

14. *Villa Pisani, Montagnana (Padova), from the* Quattro Libri, *II Book, p. 52, Venice, 1570.*

15. *Villa Pisani, 1552, Montagnana (Padova). Façade and south-west front.*

16. Villa Pisani, 1552, Montagnana (Padova). Rear façade.

17. Villa Pisani, 1552, Montagnana (Padova). Hall with four columns.

recessed between the two oval staircases, there are complete columns. Behind the house is now a walled garden. Presumably any farm buildings were placed at a distance because of the urban character of the site. The vaulted entrance, with its four columns, is a handsome feature.

The two-story portico, Doric below and Ionic above, which Thomas Jefferson planned for the earliest form of Monticello, owed much to the garden façade of the Villa Pisani.

VILLA FOSCARI, CALLED "LA MALCONTENTA"
Gambarare di Mira (Venice)

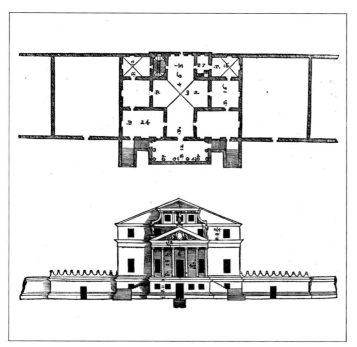

18. *Villa Foscari, Gambarare di Mira (Venice), from the* Quattro Libri, *II Book, p. 50, Venice, 1570.*
19. *Villa Foscari, 1559-1560, Gambarare di Mira (Venice). Façade.*
20. *Villa Foscari, 1559-1560, Gambarare di Mira (Venice). Rear façade.*

In the fourteenth chapter of the second book, Palladio thus described this work: "Not very far from the Gambarare, on the Brenta, is the following fabrick, belonging to the magnificent Signors Nicolò and Luigi de Foscari. This fabrick is raised eleven feet from the ground; and underneath are the kitchens, servants halls, and such like places, and vaulted above as well as below. The height of the vaults of the greater rooms, is according to the first manner for the height of vaults. The square rooms have their vaults *à cupola*. Over the small rooms there are mezzati. The vaults [sic] of the hall is crossed semi-circularly: the height of its impost, is as high as the hall is broad; which has been adorned with most excellent paintings, by Messer Battista Venetiano. Messer Battista Franco, a very great designer of our times, had begun to paint one of the great rooms; but being overtaken by death, has left the work imperfect. The loggia is of the Ionick order. The cornice goes round the house, and forms a frontispiece over the loggia; and on the opposite part below the main roof, there is another cornice, which passes over the frontispiece. The rooms above are like mezzati, by reason of their lowness; because they are but eight feet high".

As Nicolò Foscari, one of the brothers who commissioned this villa, died in 1560, and the painter Battista Franco died the following year, construction probably began not later than 1559. Although very different in appearance and plan from the Villa Pisani, that has just been described, this also is a tall structure, lacking a complement of farm buildings designed as an integral part of the villa. The Villa Foscari is essentially a suburban retreat rather than a working farm, for it is situated on the Brenta, only a short distance from Venice, and could easily be reached by boat. Consequently its main façade gave upon the river, much as if it were a palace in Venice. Because of the danger of flooding Palladio raised it high above the ground, placing the kitchens and service accommodations in a basement at ground level.

The river façade is exceptionally imposing, for there is a great projecting Ionic portico, approached by lateral stairways. It has been suggested that this feature is an adaptation of the temple of Clitumnus at Spoleto, an antique monument that Palladio had studied and described in his fourth book. Architectural orders and decoration were confined to this façade; the other three are simpler.

The chief feature of the first floor is the vaulted *salone*, in the form of a Greek cross, which is entered from the

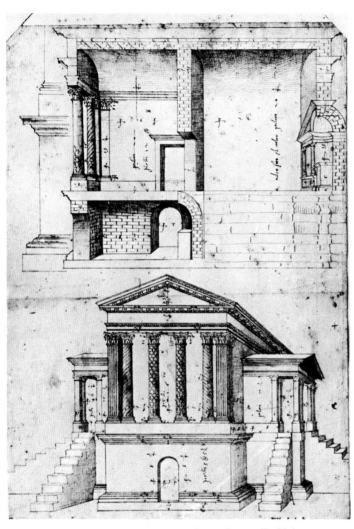

23. Temple of Clitumnus (Vicenza, Museo Civico, D 22r).

portico. On either side of the entrance arm of the *salone* are rectangular rooms and behind them square rooms. Flanking the distant arm of the cross are stairways, and at the corners of the villa smaller rectangular rooms with ceilings low enough to permit similar rooms above on a mezzanine floor. The rear façade acquires simple dignity from the great window that lights the salone, the inspiration of which came from a Roman bath. Above an eight foot high second story, there are attic rooms, lighted by dormers on the front and back of the villa.

The crenellated walls enclosing gardens on either side of the villa that appear in Palladio's plan and elevation may or may not have been built. The Villa Foscari today is free-standing on all four sides, although a later view by F. Costa showed adjacent buildings that have now disappeared. The Villa Foscari never had a great deal of land around it; unfortunately in recent years as industrialization has spread out from Mestre it is grievously hemmed up by incongruities, and has become one of the least smiling of Palladian villas. The nickname of La Malcontenta is today all too well founded.

VILLA BARBARO
Maser (Treviso)

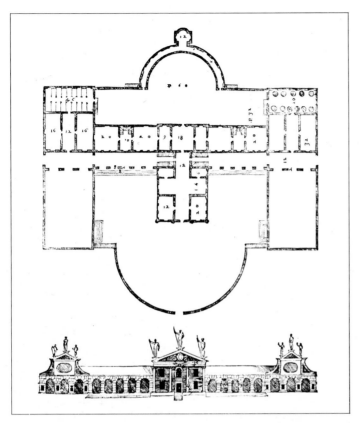

24. *Villa Barbaro, Maser (Treviso), from the* Quattro Libri, *II Book, p. 51, Venice, 1570.*
25. *Villa Barbaro, 1557-1558, Maser (Treviso). Façade, detail.*
26. *Villa Barbaro, 1557-1558, Maser (Treviso). Façade.*

During the decade of the 1550s Palladio designed this villa in Maser, near Asolo, for the noble Venetian humanist brothers, Daniele and Marc' Antonio Barbaro, both of whom have been earlier mentioned. Their property in Maser was a working farm, but as it was a principal residence for Daniele at least, it had the elegance appropriate for the home of great noblemen. Unlike most of Palladio's villas, it was set upon a hillside. Below it were the rich ploughed fields of the plain; above it were upland pastures, beyond which rose high barren mountains. Palladio took full advantage of the contours in his design. Describing it in the fourteenth chapter of book two, he wrote: "That part of the fabrick which advances a little forward, has two orders of rooms. The floor of those above is even with the level of the court backwards, where there is a fountain cut into the mountain opposite to the house, with infinite ornaments of stucco and paintings. This fountain forms a small lake, which serves for a fish-pond. From this place the water runs into the kitchen; and after having watered the gardens that are on the right and left of the road, which leads gradually to the fabrick, it forms two fish-ponds, with their watering places upon the high-road; from whence it waters the kitchen garden, which is very large, and full of the most excellent fruits, and of different kinds of pulse. The front of the master's house has four columns, of the Ionick order. The capitols of those in the angles face both ways. The method of making which capitols, I shall set down in the book of temples. On the one, and on the other hand, there are loggia's, which, in their extremities, have two dove-houses; and under them are places to make wines, the stables, and other places for the use of the villa".

The dwelling is a two-story, temple-like structure, with the Ionic columns mentioned in the previous description on the façade, which extends into the entrance courtyard. On either side are the arcades that lead to the farm dependencies. A large room in the plan of a Greek cross is entered from the central doorway in the façade. On either side of the entrance is a large rectangular room. At the other end of the building, flanking the farther arm of the cross, are smaller rooms and staircases leading to the upper floor. The villa is so placed on the hillside that the rooms in the upper story open directly on to a large rear courtyard that constitutes a secret garden, wonderfully secluded from the agricultural activities of the entrance court. A semi-circular *Nymphaeum*, with statues in niches, and elaborate ornaments is set into the hillside. A tall central

arch contains a fountain, fed by mountain streams, that flows into a pool, and on, as Palladio indicated, through the kitchens to other fishponds. All this noble elegance is in the mood of the Villa Giulia in Rome and the garden schemes and fountains that the architect Ligorio had designed at Tivoli and on the Quirinal hill for Cardinal Ippolito d'Este, to whom Daniele Barbaro had dedicated his edition of Vitruvius. These aspects of the villa clearly reflect the patron's and the architect's joint visit to Rome. Unlike the later building that was characterized as "Queen Anne in front and Maryann behind", the Villa Barbaro is a farm in front and a hidden palace behind, a thing that seldom occurs in the work of Palladio. Howard Burns has well said that Palladio was "here co-ordinating ideas, and even schemes and motifs, which were extraneous to his own vocabulary, rather than mediating largely *on his own terms* between the requirements of patrons, of site, of function, and of the principles of good architecture, as normally happens even in very complex projects for demanding employers".

The sumptuous interior decorations represent the taste of the brothers Barbaro. In the upper story mural paintings by Paolo Veronese, full of *trompe l'oeil* embellishments that multiply architectural details and place figures upon non-existent balconies, add new magnificence to admirable rooms. In the ceiling vault of the *salone*, Veronese moves up from the Veneto to Mount Olympus with the greatest of ease. Palladio says nothing whatsoever about these murals in his account of the villa.

27. *Villa Barbaro, 1557-1558, Maser (Treviso).* Nymphaeum *behind the master's house.*
28. *Villa Barbaro, 1557-1558, Maser (Treviso).* Olympus *by Paolo Veronese on* salone *vault.*
29. *Villa Barbaro, 1557-1558, Maser (Treviso).* Paintings *by Paolo Veronese in* salone.

VILLA EMO
Fanzolo (Treviso)

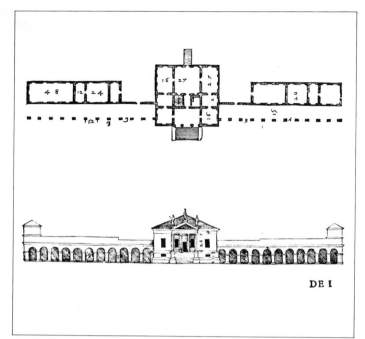

This property is an instance of the growing interest of Venetian nobles in the agricultural and economic development of the area behind Venice on the mainland. Leonardo Emo, who had had a distinguished military and administrative career in the service of the state, bought property at Fanzolo, in the region of Castelfranco, before 1535, and devoted himself to the reclamation of land, and to the establishment of mills on the Barbariga, a stream that emerged from the irrigation canal of the Brentella. He improved his fields for the growing of Indian corn, and channeled his stream to provide power for grinding his crop into polenta. Upon his death in 1559 the Fanzolo property passed to a nephew who bore his name, who undertook the construction by Palladio of the present Villa Emo in the early 1560s.

In plan this house has certain features of the Villa Barbaro: a central pavillion for the owner, with lateral *barchesse*, terminating in dove-cotes. The setting is entirely different, for the villa at Maser backed into the slope of a hill, while the Villa Emo, having been built on a plain, was surrounded by cultivated fields. Palladio's description of it in chapter fourteen of book two is laconic. "The cellars, the granaries, the stables, and the other places belonging to a villa, are on each side of the master's house; and at the extremity of each of them is a dove-house, which affords both profit to the master, and an ornament to the place; and to all which, one may go under cover: which is one of the principal things required in a villa, as has been before observed. Behind this fabrick there is a square garden of eighty *campi trevigiani*; in the middle of which runs a little river, which makes the situation very delightful and beautiful. It has been adorned with paintings by Messer Battista Venetiano".

At the Villa Barbaro the master's house, which was entered on the level of the lateral *barchesse*, projected considerably into the entrance court. At the Villa Emo the house extends only a few feet beyond the arcades of the farm buildings, but is approached by an extended ramp, leading up to a recessed loggia, the floor of which is on the level at which the arches of the *barchesse* spring. There is consequently a vaulted ground floor for the kitchens. Palladio's published plan indicates that the farm dependencies on either side are separated from the master's house by a distance equivalent to three bays of the lateral arcades; the actual distance as built was reduced to the width of a single bay. The rear of the Villa Emo is of great simplicity; here Palladio eschewed all ornament, relying solely upon proportion and the placing

32. *Villa Emo, c. 1564, Fanzolo (Treviso). Façade.*
33. *Villa Emo, c. 1564, Fanzolo (Treviso). Western* barchessa *seen from within.*
34. *Villa Emo, c. 1564, Fanzolo (Treviso). North front of the master's house and the* barchesse.

of windows for the effect. Even the windows of the main façade lack cornices. Only the recessed entrance loggia (at the top of the inclined ramp) with its Tuscan columns and sculptured pediment has architectural adornment.

However severe Palladio may have been on the exterior of the Villa Emo, Giovan Battista Zelotti (called "Battista Veneziano") who decorated the interior with allegorical mural paintings let his fancy play freely. The loggia, the vestibule, the great hall are richly decorated, as are rooms devoted to the exploits of Hercules, Venus, the Arts, Jupiter and Io, and others adorned with allegorical grotesques. The painted columns, cornices, pediments, niches of Zelotti's *trompe l'oeils* more than compensate for Palladio's restraint.

VILLA ALMERICO CAPRA,
CALLED "LA ROTONDA"
Vicenza

Palladio thus described this enchantment of his creation in chapter three of book two, which is entitled "Of the designs of town-houses", even though it is always called a villa. "Amongst many honourable Vicentine gentlemen, there is Monsignor Paolo Almerico, an ecclesiastick, and who was referendary to two supreme Popes, Pio the fourth and fifth, and who for his merit, deserved to be made a Roman citizen with all his family. This gentleman after having travelled many years out of a desire for honour, all his relations being dead, came to his native country, and for his recreation retired to one of his country-houses upon a hill, less than a quarter of a mile distant from the city, where he has built according to the following invention: which I have not thought proper to place amongst the fabricks of villa's, because of the proximity it has with the city, whence it may be said to be in the very city. The site is as pleasant and as delightful as can be found; because it is upon a small hill, of very easy access, and is watered on one side by the Bacchiglione, a navigable river; and on the other it is encompassed with most pleasant risings, which look like a very great theatre, and all are cultivated, and abound with most excellent fruits, and most exquisite vines: and therefore, as it enjoys from every part most beautiful views, some of which are limited, some more extended, and others that terminate with the horizon; there are loggia's made in all the four fronts, under the floor of which, and of the hall, are the rooms for the conveniency and use of the family. The hall is in the middle, is round, and receives its light from above. The small rooms are divided off. Over the great rooms (the vaults of which are according to the first method) there is a place to walk round the hall, fifteen foot and a half wide. In the extremity of the pedestals that form a support to the stairs of the loggia's, there are statues made by the hands of Messer Lorenzo Vicentino, a very excellent sculptor".

As the builder was a retired prelate, concerned chiefly with pleasing views from his hillside property, Palladio did not have to integrate farm buildings into the design. The villa was square, with a high basement. On each façade a broad flight of steps led to an Ionic portico with a door leading into the villa. The circular central hall on the first floor extended upward the full height of the building to a central dome, whose lantern admitted light to the apartment. In each corner of the building was a large rectangular room; four smaller rooms with lower ceilings and four hidden staircases occupied the rest of the space. On a mezzanine were four small rooms;

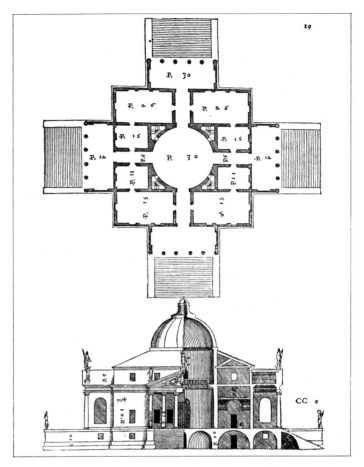

37. *Villa Rotonda, Vicenza, from the* Quattro Libri, *II Book, p. 19, Venice, 1570.*

38. *Villa Rotonda, 1566-1567, Vicenza. Northwest façade.*

40. *Villa Rotonda, 1566-1567, Vicenza. Dome of central circular hall.*
41. *Villa Rotonda, 1566-1567, Vicenza. Central circular hall.*

the low attic story was originally unfinished. The vaulted rooms of the ground story accomodated the kitchens and related offices. The plate from the *Quattro Libri* that is reproduced herewith shows a high pitched roof and dome, whereas a low pitched roof and a stepped saucer dome were actually built.

The Villa Rotonda, although supremely elegant, is neither vast in scale nor of costly construction. It is built chiefly of brick and stucco, with stone used only for the most important decorative elements. It has, however, in later centuries and other countries, inspired buildings of more grandiose scale and costly materials. Like Gabriel's Petit Trianon, it has had an endless fascination for architects of subsequent generations.

Monsignor Almerico was living in his villa in 1569; it is now thought that its construction was begun in the late 1560s. Upon his death in 1589, he bequeathed it to his illegitimate son Virginio Bartolomeo, but in 1591 the property passed to the Capra family who long retained it. Maurizio Capra, who placed his name in bold epigraphy on the entablature of the northwest portico, determined in 1591 to complete the decoration of the dome. This was painted for him by the Maganza family. The lower walls of the central hall were only frescoed far later by Luigi Dorigny.

Early in the twentieth century there was grave danger of the grounds of the Villa Rotonda being subdivided for speculative building, because of its close proximity to Vicenza. Fortunately in 1912 Count Andrea di Valmarana took possession of the property, and has not only preserved the setting of the Villa Rotonda, but has restored the depredations of time and the passing soldiery of two world wars.

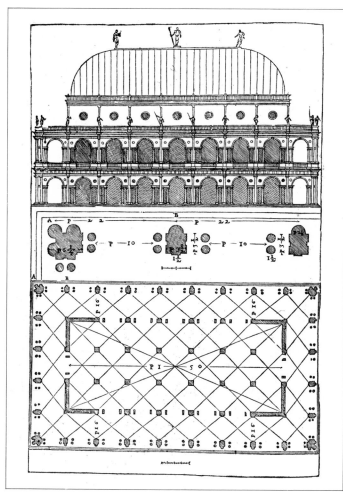

42. *The Basilica, Vicenza, from the* Quattro Libri, *II Book, p. 42, Venice, 1570.*

The Piazza dei Signori in Vicenza is adorned by two of Palladio's public designs, one executed early and the other late in his career. His first public commission was the design of the open loggias that surround the fifteenth century Palazzo della Ragione, which was the center of municipal life in Vicenza. On the ground floor of this building were municipally owned shops, rented to wool and silk merchants, booksellers, and the like, as well as the city jail; above was a great hall that served for meetings of the *Maggior Consiglio*, for the hearing of law cases, and the transaction of much public and private business. The original loggias of the palace, built between 1481 and 1494, began to collapse soon after their completion. Their repair or replacement was the subject of much discussion over several decades. In 1546 Palladio submitted a design, of which a wooden model of one bay was built. Further drawings were made, and in 1549 the Council agreed, by a vote of 99 to 17, to proceed with Palladio's design. As Palladio included plates of his design in the chapter of the third book of the *Quattro Libri* which dealt with "the Basilicas of our time", the Palazzo della Ragione has ever since been commonly known as the Basilica.

This Basilica, however, is not actually a building; it is rather a series of two-story arcades that surround and buttress a wooden-roofed Gothic hall of the previous century and the series of vaulted shops upon which that hall stands. The problem faced by Palladio was to affix a magnificent contemporary exterior, that would do credit to the aesthetic aspirations of Vicenza, to an existing structure in a way that would not impede the entrances and passageways of the earlier building. Such considerations determined the spacing of the bays of the arcades. A single arch of such width would have caused the vaults of the ground story loggia to be higher than the floor level of the hall above. To have used wide piers, with double pilasters, would have unduly darkened the arcades. Palladio solved this problem by resorting to the device of a triple opening: a central arch, supported on columns, flanked by narrower openings covered by lintels on either side. This arrangement, then called a *serliana* from its frequent appearance in the architectural books by Sebastiano Serlio, became so much a trademark of Palladio's that nearly everyone today, seeing such an arch or window, would unhesitatingly called it Palladian. By this means Palladio was able to accomodate his design to the bays imposed by the fifteenth century structure that he was envelopping. By cutting round openings

44

through the spandrels on either side of his arches, he furnished additional light in the galleries.

Work upon the arcades proceeded only as money could be spared from other city expenses. The lower level was completed on two sides by 1564, when work began upon the upper story. The Basilica was only completed in 1616. Palladio included the Basilica in the *Quattro Libri* only "because the portico's it has round it are of my invention; and because I do not doubt that the fabrick may be compared with the antient edifices, and ranked among the most noble, and most beautiful fabricks, that have been made since the antient times; not only for its grandeur, and its ornaments, but also for the materials, which is all very hard live stone, and all those stones have been joined and banded together, with the utmost diligence". Here Palladio describes his own work in superlatives; no one who has seen the Basilica in Vicenza could disagree with him.

Directly across the Piazza dei Signori is his other public masterpiece, the Loggia del Capitaniato. This too involved accommodation to previous buildings. At the end of the fourteenth century a public loggia was built in front of the former Verlato palace that had become the seat of the Capitaniato. This provided a ground floor portico that was a public meeting place, with a reception hall for the Captain above, with a balcony from which the populace in the square could be addressed. A proposal was made in 1565 to replace this building with a larger one, while in 1571 a sum was appropriated for the refashioning of the loggia. Palladio was entrusted with the work; indeed his name as architect is carved beneath the side balcony. On the principal façade was carved the name of Giambattista Bernardo, the Venetian captain in office that year. Seemingly construction was carried out between April and December 1571, for the side of the Loggia was designed in the form of a triumphal arch commemorating the victory at Lepanto on 7 October, the news of which reached Vicenza on the 18th of the same month.

The Loggia as built consisted of three bays and makes a complete unit as it stands, although it is thought that Palladio and the Council may have contemplated extending it further, perhaps to five bays. It immediately became a great ornament to the piazza by its bold magnificence. The giant order of Corinthian columns suggests imperial Rome, but the antique inspiration is modified to suit Palladio's current purposes. The windows of the upper Council chamber, for example, intrude upon the

43. *The Basilica, from the Piazza dei Signori, 1546-1549, Vicenza.*
44. *The Basilica, 1546-1549, Vicenza. Upper loggia looking toward Piazza delle Erbe.*

architrave, while to furnish further light for that apartment three windows are introduced in a kind of false-attic that rises behind the balustrade above the cornice.

As the side of the Loggia faces a narrow street, Palladio there substituted for the giant order of the principal façade smaller Corinthian columns whose architrave only reaches the level of the Council chamber floor; above is an arched window, flanked by niches, the entablatures of which create the impression of a *serliana*. On this façade the sculptor Lorenzo Rubini of Vicenza executed ornamental stuccoes commemorating the victory at Lepanto; he also embellished the main façade with military trophies and allegorical figures in the spandrels. As some of Rubini's stuccoes have disappeared, revealing the brick, there is now an element of color in the Loggia del Capitaniato that was not intended by Palladio.

45. *The Loggia del Capitaniato, 1571, Vicenza.*

THE CHIESA DEL REDENTORE
Venice

Palladio's church architecture dates from the last two decades of his life. Although he was at work on the monastery of San Giorgio Maggiore in the 1560s, he mentions it only in passing in his book of 1570. The fourth of the *Quattro Libri* is devoted to Roman temples with only the briefest reference to contemporary work. In chapter two he observes that we, "in order to observe the decorum concerning the form of temples, must chuse the most perfect, and most excellent. And since the round one is such, because it is the only one amongst all the figures that is simple, uniform, equal, strong, and capacious, let us make our temples round". In view of this preference, the only contemporary church that he illustrated was Bramante's exquisite circular tempietto of San Pietro Montorio on the Janiculum hill in Rome. The reason given was "that since Bramante was the first who brought good, and beautiful architecture to light, which from the time of the antients had been hid ... it seemed to me fit that his works should have a place among the antients".

Central plan churches, however, ill accorded with the liturgical habits of sixteenth century Italy, especially in monastic churches where a secluded choir was a requirement. So Palladio admitted that "those churches also are very laudable that are made in the form of a cross" for "they represent to the eyes of the beholders that wood from which depended our salvation", noting that of this form he had made the church of San Giorgio Maggiore in Venice. This too was the form that he adopted for the Venetian votive church of the Redentore.

The plague, which began in Venice in the late summer of 1575, killed almost a third of the population of Venice before it came to an end two years later. The fifty thousand Venetian dead amounted to more than twice the population of Vicenza. In addition to taking sanitary precautions, the Venetian Senate resolved on 4 September 1576 to build a church to the Redeemer, "not using stones of marble, but making a solid building, appropriate to a devotional church", and to go there annually on the anniversary of the end of the plague to give thanks for benefits received. A plot of land was bought on the Giudecca on 22 November 1576. Palladio had made some sketches for a central-plan church; though this form was favored by Marc' Antonio Barbaro, this was not acceptable to the Senate, which on 9 February 1577 unanimously approved "a design by our faithful Andrea Palladio in quadrangular form". The cornerstone was laid on 3 May 1577. On the following 20 July, when the plague was officially declared at an end, the Doge and Senate

46. Il Redentore, 1576-1577, Venice. Façade.
47. Il Redentore, seen from the south, 1576-1577, Venice.

47

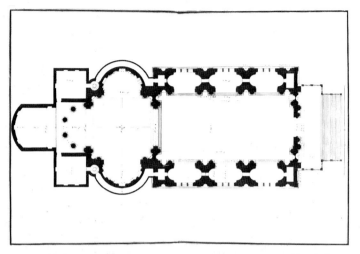

48. *Il Redentore, 1576-1577, Venice. Ground plan.*
49. *Il Redentore, 1576-1577, Venice. Nave looking from the west entrance.*

made the first of the annual pilgrimages to the site, passing over from the Zattere by a bridge of boats. The church was fifteen years in construction, being consecrated on 27 September 1592. It was entrusted to the care of the Capuchin order.

Palladio's cruciform plan provided distinct areas for the popular, the ceremonial, and the monastic functions of the church. The altar was situated in the crossing, where it could be clearly seen by the congregation in the nave, dignitaries in the transepts, and the monks in the choir. The design showed the effect of Palladio's study of the great inter-related spaces of Roman baths.

The vaulted nave of three bays was lighted by clerestory windows, semi-circular in form, divided into three sections in the manner common in baths. The side aisles were designed not for circulation but to contain chapels, three on each side. The nave and aisles were separated, and the vaults supported, by great piers, adorned (purely for decorative purposes) by pairs of giant Corinthian columns, between which were niches. The chapels were each lighted by a thermal window above the altar. This was the area designed for the congregation.

The transepts, designed to accommodate dignitaries who required a clear view of the altar, were semi-circular in plan. They did not project beyond the outside walls of the aisles, and contained no entrance doors from the outside. To provide more dignified seclusion for the occupants of the transepts, the opening from the nave to the crossing was narrowed by piers with decorative columns and niches.

The semi-circular form of the transepts was repeated in a columnar screen on the east side of the crossing. Beyond this was the monastic choir, whose occupants could be heard in the church without being seen. Over the crossing was a dome, and to the east rose two circular stair-towers that could almost pass as minarets.

The Redentore was designed to be seen from the canal. The west façade, with its two giant half-columns and two pilasters of a composite order, is an instance of Palladio's enthusiasm for adapting temple façades to current use. On the west end of the side aisles are Corinthian pilasters, which are carried around to divide the lateral walls into bays. Above the aisle roofs pairs of buttresses similarly separate the thermal windows of the clerestory. The exterior of the transepts and the choir are just plain brick, without orders or decoration of any sort. Here again one feels the inspiration of the Roman baths, where great masses of brick and concrete, quite unadorned, contribute greatly to the majesty of the building.

TEMPIETTO
Maser (Treviso)

Over the portal of this chapel is an inscription that succinctly provides the date and the names of the patron and architect: ANNO CHRISTI MDLXXX MARCUS ANTONIUS BARBARUS PROCURATOR FRANCISCI FILIUS ANDREAS PALLADIUS VICENTINO INVENTOR. Here in the town of Maser, Palladio at the very end of his life is working once again for his old patron, Marc' Antonio Barbaro, for whom more than a quarter of a century before he had designed the Villa Barbaro. Here at last the collaboration of these old allies produced a central-plan church, although on a modest scale.

The plan on the exterior is in the form of a Greek cross with very short arms. The interior space is circular, a miniature domed Pantheon, with apses for three altars, sacristies and staircases hollowed out of the masses of the walls. One enters by a six-column Corinthian portico; in the pediment is a neo-Roman relief of an unfortunate person about to lose his head; presumably St. Paul. Behind the portico rise two square small bell-towers, and behind them the stepped semi-circular dome, surmounted by a lantern. The interior is lighted from this lantern and from three thermal windows above the altar recesses. It is richly decorated with stucco ornament that recalls Palladio's patrons' taste in the *Nymphaeum* of the Villa Barbaro. Eight giant Corinthian columns are applied to the circular wall of the interior to frame the arches leading to the three altars and the entrance. Stucco angels fill the spandrels of the arches. Between these major openings are niches, framed by Corinthian columns, on the pediments of which allegorical figures recline. Stucco garlands of fruit and flowers, interspersed with heads, fill the spaces above these pediments, and decorate the entablature of the giant order that runs around the interior just below the balustrade of a narrow balcony. Only the interior of the dome is free from ornament.

Professor Ackerman writes of the Tempietto: "This irreverent child of the Pantheon is more Rococo than Roman". It is, indeed, although countless Roman elements are contained in it. I am irresistibly reminded of the *Petite Messe Solennelle* of 1863 that Gioacchino Rossini described as "one of the sins of his old age". Although originally scored for twelve singers, two pianos, and a harmonium, the composition is, in miniature, Rossini at his most exuberant, to which the word "sin" can only laughingly be applied. The Tempietto at Maser is the equivalent for Palladio. I should like to hear the Rossini *Messe Solennelle* in it.

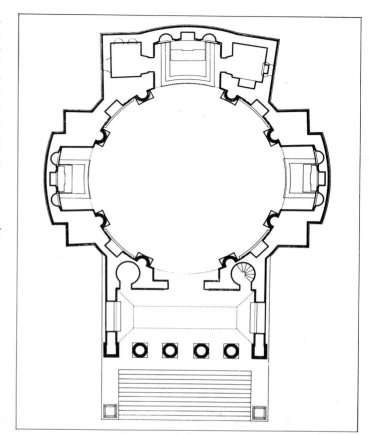

PALLADIO'S BUILDINGS
represented by photographs

VILLA GODI
Lonedo di Lugo (Vicenza)

Palladio's first villa was designed for Hieronimo Godi, a noble of Vicenza, in 1537, and was completed by 1542. It stands on a hill at Lonedo di Lugo, north of Vicenza, where the Godi family had large holdings of land and a foundry. In its height and somewhat formidable simplicity it resembles earlier country strongholds. The first floor is thirteen feet above the ground, with kitchens and offices below and granaries above. It is entered by a three-bay loggia, flanked by projecting tower-like blocks, which leads to a rectangular wooden roofed *salone*. There are four rooms in each of the blocks. The plan is completely symmetrical; the *salone* projects from the rear façade just as the loggia is recessed on the entrance side. The relation of the loggia and towers somewhat recalls the Villa Trissino, on which Palladio had worked, but at the Villa Godi there are no orders or pediments; the exterior is of stark simplicity. The material was brick, covered with stucco, as was usual in Palladio's villas. The various arcades and outbuildings shown in the plan in the *Quattro Libri* were not constructed; they probably represent a scheme by which Palladio's earliest work might have been brought more closely into harmony with his later ideas.

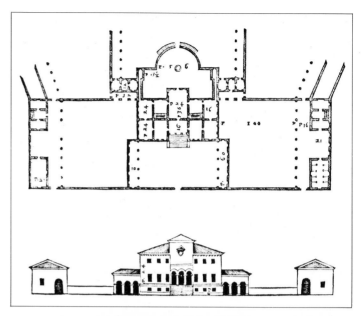

55. *Villa Godi, Lonedo di Lugo (Vicenza), from the* Quattro Libri, *II Book, p. 75, Venice, 1570.*
56. *Villa Godi, 1537, Lonedo di Lugo (Vicenza). General view from above.*

57. Villa Godi, 1537, Lonedo di Lugo (Vicenza). Entrance loggia.

VILLA VALMARANA
Vigardolo di Monticello Co. Otto (Vicenza)

This villa, begun in 1541 for Giuseppe Valmarana, corresponds exactly in ground plan to a Palladio drawing in the Royal Institute of British Architects (XVII/2), although in construction the upper part of the design was clumsily altered. It is of interest as Palladio's second villa, and the first that he built after his return from Rome in 1541. Although it stands on a podium, approached by a broad staircase, it hugs the ground, as the Villa Godi did not. The rooms are symmetrically grouped, much as in the Villa Trissino. The façade in the plan was marked by the *serliana* that gave access to the loggia, and by a divided pediment that was omitted in the actual building. The plan called for groin vaults, a feature that had entranced Palladio in the Roman baths, in the loggia and the two front rooms.

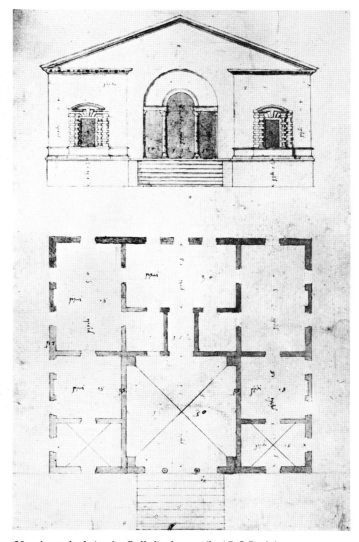

58. *An early design by Palladio for a villa (R.I.B.A.).*

VILLA MARCELLO
Bertesina (Vicenza)

This villa, built about 1542 for a salt tax collector who had invested his profits in land, was not described by Palladio in the *Quattro Libri*, although two of his plans for it are in the Royal Institute of British Architects (XVII/27, XVI/16a). The first shows a single-story villa, raised sufficiently from the ground to allow for kitchens below with a central loggia, leading into a rectangular *salone* parallel to it, with three windows on either side. In a subsequent plan, and in construction, the size was reduced, bringing the façade from nine bays to seven, and creating an L-shaped *salone*. The elaborate vaulting systems of the first plan were eliminated, while the Ionic half-columns shown on the façade were replaced by composite pilasters.

60, 61. Villa Marcello, Bertesina (Vicenza). Preliminary drawings (R.I.B.A.).
62. Villa Marcello, c. 1542, Bertesina (Vicenza). Façade.

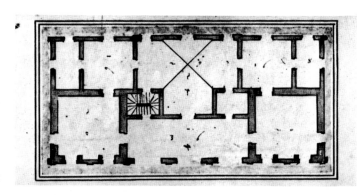

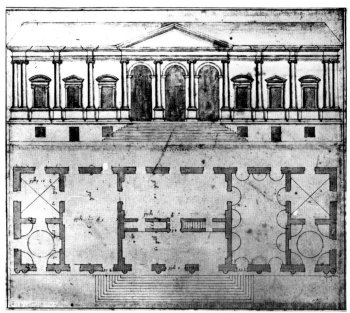

VILLA PISANI
Bagnolo di Lonigo (Vicenza)

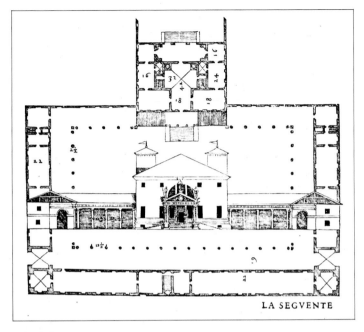

LA SEGVENTE

This villa, which was among Palladio's early commissions after his return from Rome in 1541, was his first work for a noble family of Venice. Giovanni Pisani had bought this property in the territory of Vicenza in 1523, together with a house that had belonged to Girolamo Nogarola. Palladio was commissioned by the Counts Vittore, Marco, and Daniele Pisani, sons of Giovanni, to design a replacement for Nogarola's house, which he completed by 1544.

Overlooking the river was a three-bay loggia, with rusticated Doric stone pilasters, flanked by two towers that recalled the *castello* that had earlier been on the site. A groin vaulted *salone*, cruciform in plan, extended through the house from the loggia to the entrance façade, with a thermal window over the entrance. The entrance portico and lateral L-shaped arcades shown in the plan in the *Quattro Libri* were not built, although Palladio subsequently built in the 1560s a Doric farm court for the villa. The Villa Pisani's main floor stood some seven feet above the ground, with kitchens below and granaries above.

63. *Villa Pisani, Bagnolo di Lonigo (Vicenza), from the* Quattro Libri, *II Book, p. 47, Venice, 1570.*
64. *Villa Pisani, 1542-1545, Bagnolo di Lonigo (Vicenza). Rear façade overlooking river.*

59

VILLA CALDOGNO
Caldogno (Vicenza)

The disposition of the façade of the Villa Caldogno closely resembles that of the Villa Saraceno of 1545. The rusticated stone work of the loggia, although without pilasters, recalls the Villa Pisani that has just been described. Although there is no documentation for this building, it logically falls in with Palladio's villas of the 1540s. Although the plan is simpler and the central room is not vaulted, the villa is richly decorated with mural paintings by Fasolo. An inscription on the façade with the name of the owner, Angelo, son of Losco, Caldogno and the date 1570 refers more probably to his succession to the property, or to the completion of the decoration, than to the date of construction of the villa.

65. *Villa Caldogno, c. 1545, Caldogno (Vicenza). View from the east.*

60

VILLA THIENE
Quinto Vicentino (Vicenza)

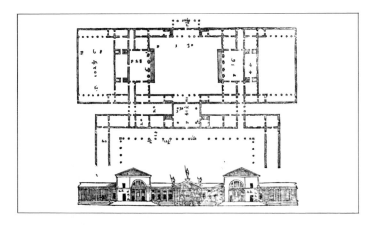

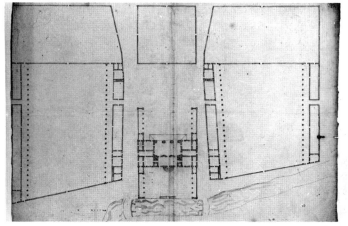

In the *Quattro Libri* Palladio published a design for a great villa, representing his ideas for adapting a Roman house to sixteenth century use, that would have permitted Count Ottavio Thiene to expand a more modest structure begun about 1545-46 by his father, Count Marc' Antonio, and his uncle, Count Adriano Thiene. This grandiose enlargement was never achieved. All that remains today is a building that bears some relation to the pavilion to the right of the inner court in the published plan; this now serves as the town hall of Quinto Vicentino. A drawing at Worcester College, Oxford, not by Palladio, shows this structure as part of a simpler plan, with symmetrical walled enclosures beyond the streets that pass on either side of the villa on their way to river crossings.

66. *Villa Thiene, Quinto Vicentino (Vicenza), from the* Quattro Libri, *II Book, p. 64, Venice, 1570.*
67. *Villa Thiene, Quinto Vicentino (Vicenza). A proposed plan (Worcester College, Oxford).*
68. *Villa Thiene, c. 1545-1546, Quinto Vicentino (Vicenza). Rear façade.*

69. *Villa Thiene, c. 1545-1546, Quinto Vicentino (Vicenza). Façade.*

VILLA POJANA
Pojana Maggiore (Vicenza)

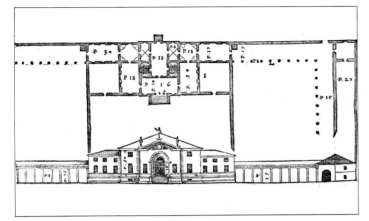

In this house, built about 1549 for Bonifacio Pojana, the façade recalls Palladio's earlier Villa Valmarana, although here the *serliana* in the center has five *oculi*, in the manner of Bramante's *Nymphaeum* at Gennezzano, to admit more light to the entrance loggia, and small attic windows are introduced below the cornice. The villa, being raised five feet above the ground, has kitchens and storerooms below the main floor; granaries were in the attic. The vaulted rooms, of different sizes and heights, were handsomely decorated by the Veronese painters Anselmo Camera and Bernardino India. The lateral arcades shown in the *Quattro Libri* were not built.

70. Villa Pojana, Pojana Maggiore (Vicenza), from the Quattro Libri, *II Book, p. 58, Venice, 1570.*

71. Villa Pojana, 1548-1549, Pojana Maggiore (Vicenza). Façade and south wall.

VILLA CORNARO
Piombino Dese (Treviso)

The Villa Cornaro, with the previously described Villa Pisani in Montagnana, represents a new departure in Palladio's style: the two-story villa with superimposed porticos decorating the façade. At Montagnana a Doric order decorates the lower story with its entablature carried around the building, while the upper order is Ionic. In the Villa Cornaro Ionic is used below and Corinthian above. As the Villa Pisani fronts directly upon a street, the double portico of the entrance consists of columns engaged to the façade. The Villa Cornaro being approached through grounds, the porticos project from the façade. The villas have identical treatments of the rear façades: columned loggias recessed into the façade, with oval staircases on either side. As both villas were designed for Venetian families, Palladio may well have been following the taste of his clients in the superimposed loggias, which were to be found in palaces in Venice.

The Cornaro family's land holdings in Piombino dated from the fifteenth century. On the death of Girolamo Cornaro in 1551 the property was inherited by his two sons, the younger of whom, Giorgio Cornaro, commissioned Palladio to design this villa. Construction apparently began soon after, for it was inhabited in 1554, although not completely finished for some years. The Villa Cornaro has modest wings on either side of the main façade, but no extensive group of outbuildings.

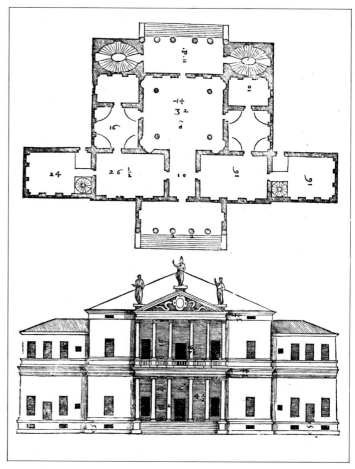

72. *Villa Cornaro, Piombino Dese (Vicenza), from the* Quattro Libri, *II Book, p. 53, Venice, 1570.*

73. *Villa Cornaro, 1553, Piombino Dese (Vicenza). Rear façade from the garden.*

VILLA BADOER
Fratta Polesine (Rovigo)

The Venetian noble Francesco Badoer, who had inherited land in Fratta Polesine, commissioned Palladio to build him a villa there about 1556. The property stood above the Scortico river, a branch of the Adige, from which it could conveniently be reached by water from Venice. The ground plan of the main floor resembled that of the Villa Pojana, but the effect of the two houses was very different, for the Villa Badoer had an impressive six-column Ionic portico, stood higher above the ground, and had a forecourt with curved arcades in the form of a quarter circle on either side of the broad steps that led up to the portico. At the Villa Barbaro arcades extended laterally on either side of the house at the same level. But here the master's house is set conspicuously above the dependencies; the eye of anyone approaching from the river is subtly carried thither by the curving arcades. Although Palladio on other occasions put such curved arcades in his projects, the Villa Badoer seems to be the single instance in which they were built.

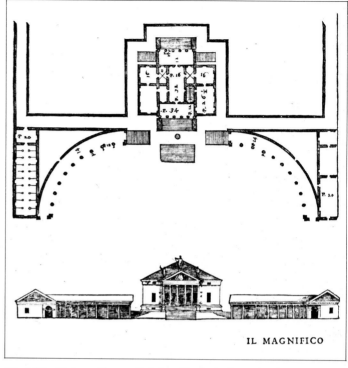

IL MAGNIFICO

74. *Villa Badoer, Fratta Polesine (Rovigo),* from the Quattro Libri, *II Book, p. 48, Venice, 1570.*

75. *Villa Badoer, 1556, Fratta Polesine (Rovigo). Forecourt and façade.*

VILLA ZENO
Donegal di Cessalto (Treviso)

The plan for this villa probably dates from about 1559 when its builder, Marco Zeno, a Venetian nobleman, was made Podestà of Vicenza. Only the central block was built; that was completed about 1566. The façade, with a triple arched loggia, is related to those of the Villas Saraceno and Caldogno; the high *salone*, once lit by a thermal window, recalls the Villa Pisani at Bagnolo. The arcades and outbuildings called for in the *Quattro Libri* plan, were never constructed, while the façades of the master's house have been drastically remodelled, to their detriment.

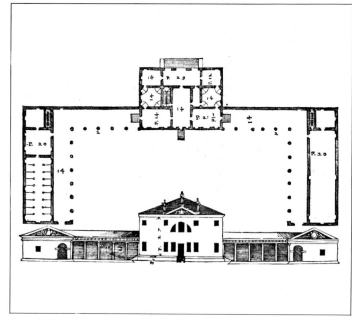

76. *Villa Zeno, Donegal di Cessalto (Treviso), from the* Quattro Libri, *II Book, p. 49, Venice, 1570.*

VILLA SAREGO
Santa Sofia di Pedemonte (Verona)

This house outside of Verona, designed for Marc' Antonio Sarego, is a maverick among the villas of Palladio. As it is dated around 1569, it is the last one that he did. It was grandiosely conceived and only partly built, in a style quite different from his other work. As conceived, a U-shaped arcaded forecourt with stables led to the entrance to an enclosed courtyard, around which the master's house was to be built. This inner court was edged by an arcade of giant rusticated columns with Ionic capitals with balconies inside it at the level of the piano nobile. Only the left half of this inner court was ever built. The plan, which differs so startlingly from Palladio's other villas, apparently represented an effort to adapt the arrangement of an ancient Roman villa to sixteenth century Italian life. It proved too grandiose to be practical.

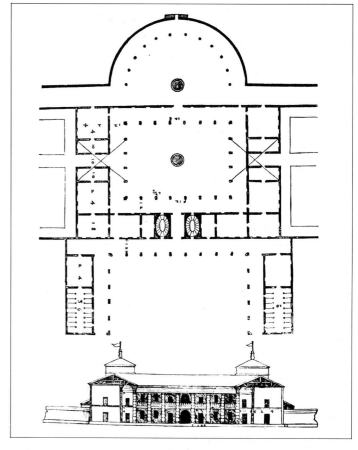

78. *Villa Sarego, Santa Sofia di Pedemonte (Verona), from the* Quattro Libri, *II Book, p. 67, Venice, 1570.*
79. *Villa Sarego, c. 1569, Santa Sofia di Pedemonte (Verona). Only executed part of courtyard.*

VILLA TRISSINO
Meledo di Sarego (Vicenza)

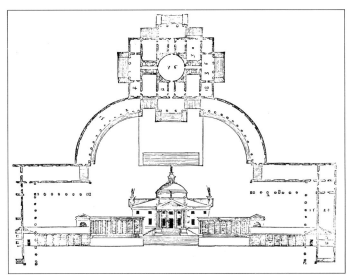

81, 82. *Villa Trissino, Meledo di Sarego (Vicenza). Model.*

83. *Villa Trissino, Meledo di Sarego (Vicenza), from the* Quattro Libri, *II Book, p. 60, Venice, 1570.*

84. *Villa Trissino, 1567, Meledo di Sarego (Vicenza). All that was built.*

The Villa Trissino was the the most grandiose of Palladio's projects; even less was achieved than at the Villa Sarego, for all that exists at Meledo is a barn with Tuscan columns and a tower. The project was said to have been "begun" in 1566, but in the *Quattro Libri* four years later Palladio still used the future tense in giving this description: "The following fabrick was begun by Count Francesco, and Count Lodovico di Trissini, brothers, at Meledo, a village in the Vicentine. The situation is very beautiful, because it is upon a hill, which is washed by an agreeable little river, in the middle of a very spacious plain, and near to a well frequented road. Upon the summit of the hill, there is to be a round hall, encompassed with the rooms, but so high, that it may receive its light from above them. There are some half columns in the hall, that support a gallery, into which one goes from the rooms above; which by reason they are but seven feet high, serve for mezzati. Under the floor of the first rooms, there are the kitchens, servant's halls, and other places. And because every front has a very beautiful prospect, there are four loggia's, of the Corinthian order; above the frontispiece of which the cupola of the hall rises. The loggia's that tend to the circumference, form an agreeable prospect. Nearer to the plan, are the haylofts, the cellars, the stables, the granaries, the places for the farmer, and other rooms for the use of the villa. The columns of these portico's are of the Tuscan order. Over the river, in the angles of the court, are two dovehouses".

It is as if one enlarged the Villa Rotonda, adding from the entrance portico lateral flights of steps leading down to curving quarter-circle arcades, as at the Villa Badoer, at the conclusion of which still more steps lead down to an even larger forecourt, surrounded by farm buildings. The expense of this would have daunted even as enthusiastic patrons as the Trissini. Although the villa was never built, a 1:33 scale model was constructed for the 1973 exhibition in Vicenza, which translated into three dimensions the illustration of the *Quattro Libri*.

The last illustration in the second book of the *Quattro Libri* represents still another unachieved extravaganza– a villa proposed for Leonardo Mocenigo at a site that he owned on the Brenta. Here, as in the Villa Thiene and the Villa Sarego, an illusion of an ancient house was to be created by means of an inner court, around which the master's lodgings were to extend. The court, like the building that surrounded it, was square. Giant porticos were on all four faces of the house; on two sides these were reached by curved arcades that concealed dependencies. It was an admirable piece of elegant symmetry, but once again beyond the range of possibility. But it is still another instance of Palladio's delight in investigating the life of the ancient world and trying to adapt a Roman villa to the contemporary scene.

PALAZZO CIVENA
Vicenza

This, which was Palladio's first city palace, was built in 1540-1542. Although it was completed before his first trip to Rome, much of its inspiration came from Bramante's design of 1513 for the House of Raphael, which Palladio must have known through his association with Trissino and the building of the villa at Cricoli. The palace façade is of five bays, without any central emphasis. On the ground story is an open arcade for the convenience of pedestrians; the bays of the upper floor are defined by paired Corinthian pilasters. The greater part of the ground floor is devoted to a cruciform vaulted atrium, running through the building, according to a manuscript drawing owned by the Royal Institute of British Architects (XVII/14). The Palazzo Civena is simple and restrained, but it is the earliest example of the classical style to be built in Vicenza.

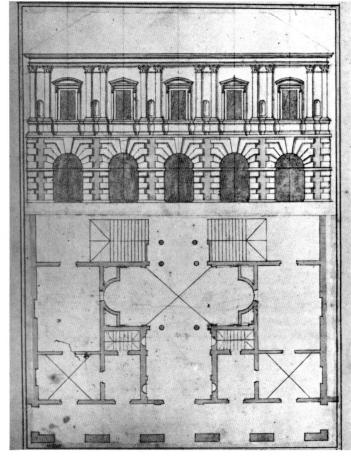

85. Palazzo Civena, Vicenza. Palladio's preliminary drawing (R.I.B.A.)

86. Palazzo Civena, 1540-1542, Vicenza. Façade.

PALAZZO THIENE
Vicenza

The enlargement of Palladio's horizons in a short time is strikingly shown by the grandiosity of this palace that he designed for the brothers Marc' Antonio and Ottavio Thiene immediately after the completion of the Palazzo Civena. The Palazzo Thiene was designed to fill an entire block, fronting on the main street of Vicenza. The scale and magnificence of its conception could only be likened to the Cancelleria and Farnese palaces in Rome. It was to be built around a great open court, with the piano nobile conspicuously taller than the ground floor. The rustication of the lower story of the façades, of the piers in the *cortile*, and the rough columns of the vestibule, as well as the windows of the *piano nobile*, all recall the work of Giulio Romano, who may possibly have had some hand in the design.

The contract for the building was drawn on 10 October 1542 between Palladio, described as a stonemason, Marc' Antonio Thiene, and three builders. The work was never finished, for only a quarter was actually constructed, but what a stupendous fragment it is! The construction of this portion must have occupied fifteen years, for Alessandro Vittoria was engaged in decorating the palace in 1552-1553, and dates of 1556 and 1558 are inscribed on the exterior and in the *cortile*, respectively, presumably indicating the years of completion. The great rooms of the *piano nobile* are adorned with a richness of paintings and stucco decoration that are worthy of the magnificence of the architecture. The palace is now admirably maintained by the Banca Popolare di Vicenza.

87. *Palazzo Thiene, 1542 and 1546, Vicenza. Façade of the only corner completed.*

76

88. *Palazzo Thiene, Vicenza, from the* Quattro Libri, *II Book, p. 13, Venice, 1570.*
89. *Location in Vicenza of the Palazzo Thiene (right) and Palazzo Barbaran da Porto; only sections in black were built.*
90. *Palazzo Thiene, 1542 and 1546, Vicenza. Interior courtyard.*

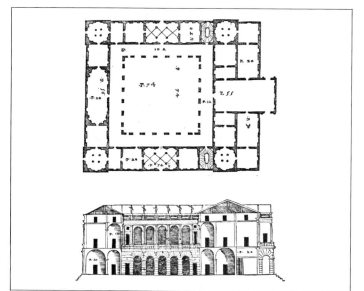

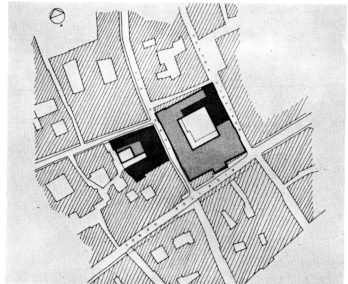

PALAZZO DA PORTO FESTA
Vicenza

Although not precisely documented, this palace presumably dates from around 1549 when Iseppo Porto married Livia, the sister of Marc' Antonio Thiene. As the lot chosen was a rectangular one with frontage on two streets, Palladio proposed palace blocks, with identical façades, on both streets — one for the master and his ladies and the other for guests, who would thus have freedom of action — that would be connected by a great interior courtyard. The façades, rusticated below with an Ionic order above, still recalled Bramante's House of Raphael. The courtyard, however, was to be surrounded by a giant composite order, with a gallery at the level of the *piano nobile*. The plan was never completely carried out, for only the master's part of the house was built. Although the giant composite order never adorned the courtyard, Palladio used this motif two decades later in his design of the Villa Sarego.

As the palace fronted on a narrow street, and could not be seen from a distance, the seven bays of the façade were designed to look their best at close range. To give variety, sculptured ornament was used around the windows of the first floor in the central and end bays.

In order of construction, Palladio's next design for a palace in Vicenza was the Chiericati, which has already been described.

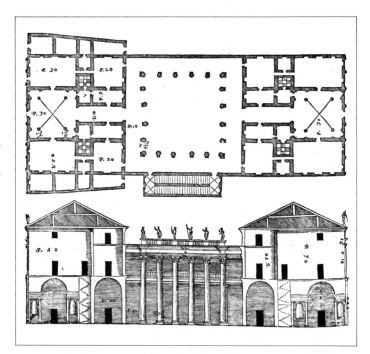

91. *Palazzo da Porto Festa, Vicenza, from the* Quattro Libri, *II Book, p. 8, Venice, 1570.*
92. *Palazzo da Porto Festa, c. 1549, Vicenza. Atrium.*

93. *Palazzo da Porto Festa, c. 1549, Vicenza. Façade.*

PALAZZO ANTONINI
Udine

Palladio's collaboration with Monsignor Daniele Barbaro led to his receiving commissions not only in Venice but in other parts of the Veneto. Having met, through Barbaro, Floriano Antonini, the Friulian representative in Venice, Palladio made a visit to Udine in 1556, and designed this palace, which was the first to be illustrated in book two of the *Quattro Libri*.

Essentially it is a later and enlarged version of the Villa Pisani at Montagnana and the Villa Cornaro, although built in a town. As in these villas, the front and rear façades have a double order, with a portico at the back. In Udine, however, the ground floor Ionic order is rusticated, as are the quoins and the ground floor windows. The main door leads into an atrium with four columns, over which is placed the *salone*. As there was open space on one side of the palace, Palladio proposed an asymmetrical wing to house the kitchen; this, however, was never built.

The appearance of the Palazzo Antonini is today gravely marred by a very un-Palladian roof, useful for coping with snow but lethal to the original design. If a gentleman in evening dress were to clamp upon his head a straw hat borrowed from a farmer's horse, the effect would be similar. The extended eaves of this roof seem to come down over the ears and eyes of the palace.

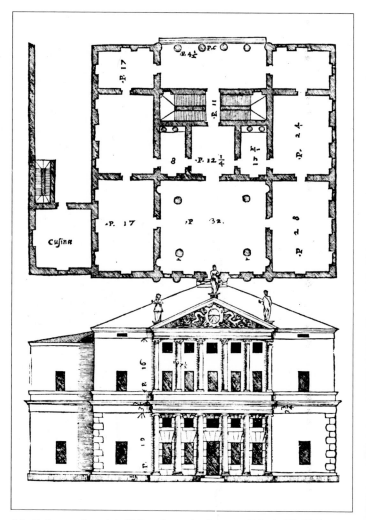

94. *Palazzo Antonini, Udine, from the* Quattro Libri, *II Book, p. 5, Venice, 1570.*

95. *Palazzo Antonini, 1556, Udine.*

PALAZZO VALMARANA BRAGA
Vicenza

The Valmarana family having owned property on this site in the center of Vicenza since 1487, Palladio designed a ·new palace in 1565-1566 for the widowed Isabella Nogarola Valmarana. Although the street on which it faces (now Corso Fogazzaro) is narrow, it curves sufficiently to allow a view of this particular site from a distance. Consequently Palladio designed a bold façade with six giant pilasters and a heavy cornice that command this distant view. The podium of this giant order is high, with rusticated quoins; between its pilasters are, in each bay, smaller ones that rise only to the floor level of the *piano nobile*. At the ends of the façade the giant pilasters are omitted, so that sculptured caryatids may take their places. There is a larger-than-life quality about the whole design.

A long rectangular entrance led to a loggia with Ionic columns, over which the *salone* was placed on the first floor, overlooking a spacious garden court. Only this front block of the palace was built. The matching loggia on the far side of the court, the rooms along the lateral walls, and the dependencies and stables at the far end of Palladio's plan were never constructed. The Palazzo Valmarana, which had suffered greatly during World War II, was subsequently bought and restored by Dr. Vittor Luigi Braga Rosa. For a number of years the Centro Internazionale di Studi di Architettura Andrea Palladio was pleasantly housed on the first floor of this palace, before moving to its present quarters in the Domus Comestabilis at the Basilica Palladiana.

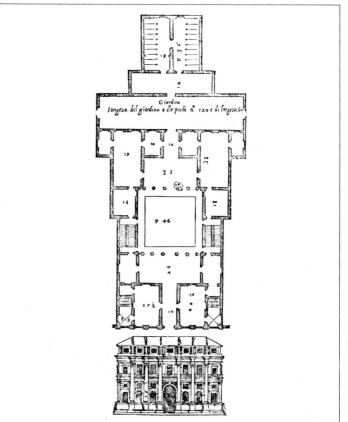

82

PALAZZO BARBARAN DA PORTO
Vicenza

Count Montano Barbarano had difficulty in finding a suitable site for this palace. Before 1570 Palladio designed him a palace for an irregular plot that he had bought in the block next to the Palazzo Thiene. Seemingly construction had begun on the plan published in the *Quattro Libri*, which showed a seven-bay façade with a giant order, leading through a vaulted entrance with four columns, to a modest *cortile* with a three bay loggia. When Barbarano succeeded in buying more street frontage, Palladio altered the plan, explaining to the readers of his book that the development was so recent that there had been no time to have a new one engraved.

As built, the façade is of nine bays, with the entrance off center. Instead of the giant order, there is a double one, Ionic below and Corinthian above, and the façade is richly ornamented. The courtyard was greatly increased in size, and was to be surrounded by a colonnade. However only one side of this loggia was built, and the enlarged plan remained not only problematical but unfinished.

99. Palazzo Barbaran da Porto, 1569-1570, Vicenza. Façade.

100. *Palazzo Barbaran da Porto, Vicenza, from the* Quattro Libri, *II Book, p. 22, Venice, 1570.*

101. *Palazzo Barbaran da Porto, 1569-1570, Vicenza. Atrium.*
102. *Palazzo Barbaran da Porto, 1569-1570, Vicenza. Ground plan.*

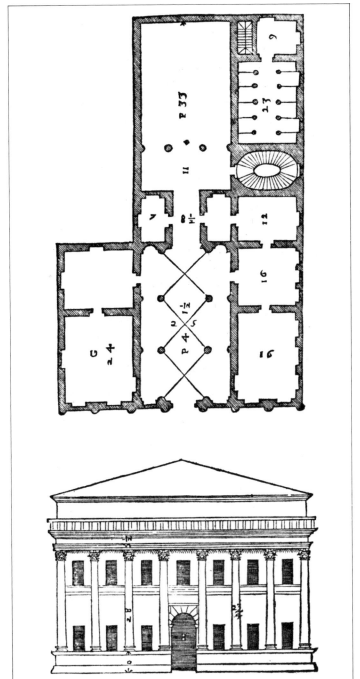

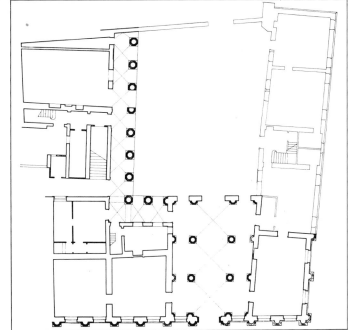

PALAZZO DA PORTO BREGANZE
Vicenza

As this appealing fragment was designed after 1570 when Palladio published his book, his precise intentions are not clear. What we have is two bays of a palace for Alessandro da Porto, with a gigantic order, resting on so high a podium that the columns only start at the top of the ground story windows. Between the capitals are carved garlands; attic windows peer out of a heavy cornice. As the palace stood on a square, Palladio clearly designed it to be seen from a distance without loss of detail. This was Palladio's last Vicenza palace design, although Vincenzo Scamozzi built the fragment of it that was completed. A later reconstruction drawing by Francesco Muttoni suggests that this was to be a palace with a façade of seven bays, with a central entrance, vaulted, with four columns, leading to a courtyard with a double order. If completed, it would have been a noble climax to Palladio's series of Vicenza palaces, which were more often than not designed for patrons whose eyes and imagination outran even their substantial purses. Even as a fragment, like isolated columns in the Roman Forum, it suggests the majesty of the city that Palladio sought to create.

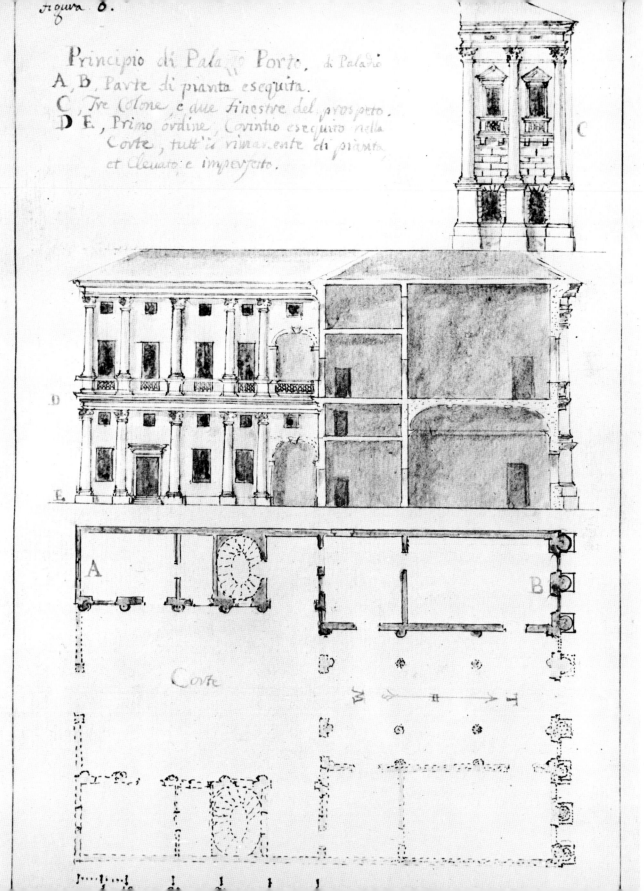

figura 8.

Principio di Pala__o Porto, di Paladio
A, B, Parte di pianta esequita.
C, Tre Colone e due finestre del prospeto.
D E, Primo ordine, Corintio esequito nella
     Corte, tutt'il rimanente di pianta
     et elevato, e imperfeto.

A

Corte

B

PALAZZO THIENE BONIN-LONGARE
Vicenza

At the beginning of the Corso Palladiano in Vicenza, behind the Porta Castello, stands the Palazzo Bonin-Longare, whose date and authorship have been much discussed. It is claimed that Palladio designed it for a member of the Thiene family, although it has also been attributed to Vincenzo Scamozzi. The proportions of the façade are unusual, for the ground story with its engaged columns is higher than was Palladio's wont, and indeed appears to be taller than the *piano nobile*, which also has its order. The façade is of seven bays, with a central entrance; on the rear are superimposed loggias. As this palace is not mentioned in Palladio's *Quattro Libri*, it seems that the design must be later than 1570, if indeed he had a hand in it.

105. *Palazzo Thiene Bonin-Longare, after 1572, Vicenza. Courtyard.*
106. *Palazzo Thiene Bonin-Longare, after 1572, Vicenza. Façade.*

THE CONVENT OF THE CARITÀ
Venice

The design that Palladio furnished for a new convent of the Carità in Venice in the 1560s represented his attempt to adapt his conception of an ancient Roman house to monastic use. From the existing fifteenth century church's south aisle a door would lead to a Corinthian atrium with a giant order whose columns were thirty-five feet tall. From the east gallery of this opened the sacristy, called by Palladio the *tablinum*, in recollection of the room where ancient Romans lodged the images of their ancestors. A door in the south wall of the atrium gave upon the cloister, where three orders superimposed expressed the three floors of the building. The lower gallery had a Doric order, an upper gallery the Ionic, while on the top level, where there were rooms with windows above the lower arcades, was a Corinthian order. Further to the south was projected a refectory, as high as the third order of the cloister, with a loggia on each side.

Only part of this plan was carried out, and much of what was built was destroyed by fire. The convent having been secularized, the remains of Palladio's work now form part of the Accademia di Belle Arti. A vaulted sacristy with two columns and two exedrae for statues, an adjacent oval stone staircase, and a single side of the cloister (with the open arcades disfigured by subsequent glazing) are all that survive of Palladio's great design. Goethe, having hurried off to the Carità on 2 October 1786 soon after his arrival in Venice, wrote: "Alas, scarcely a tenth of it has been built, but even this little is worthy of the divine genius. I am convinced I am right when I say that I never saw anything more sublime, more perfect, in my life. One ought to spend years contemplating such a work". He was especially charmed by what he deemed "the most beautiful winding staircase in the world". "This has a broad open newel and the stone steps are built into the wall and so tiered that each supports the one above it. How beautifully it is constructed can be gathered from the fact that Palladio himself was satisfied with it".

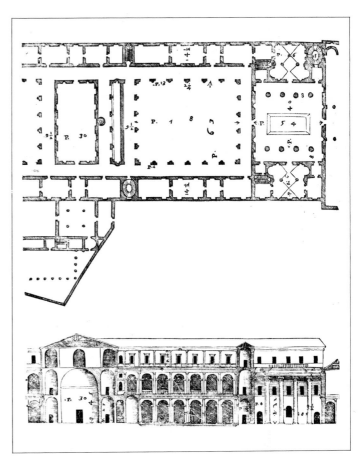

107. Convent of the Carità, Venice, from the Quattro Libri, *II Book, p. 30, Venice, 1570.*

108. Convent of the Carità, 1560-1561, Venice. Cloister.

SAN FRANCESCO DELLA VIGNA
Venice

At the Carità, Palladio had been designing monastic buildings, a process that was a simple extension of his earlier work with villas and palaces. When commissioned in 1562 to create a façade for the Venetian church of San Francesco della Vigna, built nearly three decades earlier from the designs of Jacopo Sansovino, he attacked for the first time the problems of church architecture.

There had never been an obvious solution to the problem of designing a west façade for a church, built in the basilican tradition, that had a high central nave covered by a gable roof, that was flanked by one or more lower aisles on either side. How was one to adapt the conventional classical portico to such a structure and still have it reflect the nature of the building that it adorned?

Palladio's solution was to apply four Corinthian columns of a giant order to the west wall of the nave and to treat it as one temple. To each of the aisles he applied a smaller Corinthian order, surmounted by half a pediment that expressed the lower height of these parts of the church. This smaller order was repeated on either side of the entrance in the center, which was surmounted by a thermal window. To tie the three parts together he carried the entablature of the smaller order of the aisles façade behind the giant columns of the nave façade. It is as if he had designed a big and a little temple, split the smaller one down the middle and attached the parts to either side of the big one; a simple enough solution in retrospect, but in 1562 a revolutionary one, for Palladio's predecessors had not found the way to adapt a classical temple portico to the west end of a basilica.

112. *San Francesco della Vigna, 1562, Venice. Façade.*

SAN GIORGIO MAGGIORE
Venice

The Benedictine monastery on the Isola San Giorgio, across the water from the Doge's Palace and the Piazza San Marco, began about 1520 to contemplate the rebuilding of its church and most of its monastic buildings. In 1560 Palladio was brought in to complete the work on a new refectory, begun twenty years earlier. His task was to complete the vaults for a long room about 10 meters wide and 30 long, for which the walls were substantially built. He covered this area with a barrel vault into which entered cross vaults that rose above the two thermal windows that he introduced into each of the lateral walls. When the work was completed in 1563, Paolo Veronese's *Marriage at Cana* was placed on the end wall, with a thermal window above it.

Palladio was soon charged with the design of a new church for the monastery, upon which construction was begun in 1566. The white marble façade, which represented the solution that he had earlier achieved at San Francesco della Vigna, became the dominating feature of the island and one of the trade-marks of Venice. The exterior of the church otherwise was of brick. The interior had many of the characteristics used a decade later in the Redentore, although here the aisles were relatively wider, the transepts extended beyond the outside walls of the aisles, while the sanctuary and monk's choir were considerably longer than the nave. In keeping with Venetian tradition, Palladio placed a dome over the crossing. The church was substantially finished by 1576, but the façade was not completed until the second decade of the following century.

113. *San Giorgio Maggiore, 1565, Venice. View from the air, refectory on right.*
114. *San Giorgio Maggiore, 1565, Venice. Façade.*

TEATRO OLIMPICO
Vicenza

At the very end of his life, Andrea Palladio had the opportunity to put into practice his studies of Roman theatres and amphitheatres. The Accademia Olimpica in Vicenza in 1579 resolved to build a permanent theatre. In May 1580 they were granted a site near the Piazza Chiericati and the Ponte degli Angeli, the shape of which prompted Palladio to propose a half-amphitheatre plan rather than a semicircular one. His design, which must have been completed by May 1580, provided an elaborately decorated proscenium, with an arched central opening and smaller side ones, through which architectural sets could be seen. Rows of steps for the spectators were terminated at the top by an arcade, the floor of which was at the level of the entablature of the lower order of the proscenium.

While construction was proceeding on its slow course, in August 1580 Palladio died. By 1583 the stage front had been finished but there were no sets. When Vincenzo Scamozzi was asked to design these in 1584, he made some alterations in Palladio's design to accommodate the theatre director's ideas of staging. Finally the Teatro Olimpico opened on 3 March 1585 with the performance of a contemporary translation of Sophocles' *Oedipus Rex*.

With the Teatro Olimpico we come to the end of works by Palladio begun in his lifetime. To conclude on a note of triumph, I add, in the nature of a colophon, a photograph of the Arco delle Scalette at the entrance to the long staircase that led from Vicenza to the hillside sanctuary of Monte Berico. It was built only in 1595, fifteen years after Palladio's death, but local tradition attributes the design to him.

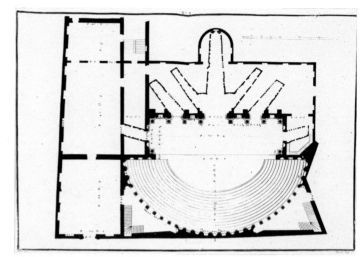

119. *Teatro Olimpico, 1580, Vicenza. Ground plan.*
120. *Teatro Olimpico, 1580, Vicenza. Proscenium.*

121. *Teatro Olimpico, 1580, Vicenza. Center of proscenium.*

122. *Teatro Olimpico, 1580. Vicenza. Proscenium and seats.*
123. *Teatro Olimpico, 1580, Vicenza. Seats and upper arcade.*

124. *Arco delle Scalette, 1576 (?), Vicenza.*

PALLADIO IN AMERICA
by Frederick Doveton Nichols

Palladio, the great sixteenth century master who lived near Venice, was the most influential single architect who ever lived. The Europeans have always been great admirers of his work, and through their over-seas colonies his influence became world wide. But in Britain, particularly, his drawings were carefully studied, since they had been purchased by Inigo Jones from the heirs of Palladio only 32 years after his death in 1580. His great book, the *Quattro Libri*, was studied in detail. Through the enthusiasm of the Earl of Burlington, Palladianism in England became a cult, based chiefly upon his drawings and books, due to the inaccessibility of the buildings in the Veneto.

Because of Palladio's abilities, scholars of many nations have become enchanted with his art, and have sought the secret of his enormous influence. To begin with, the *Quattro Libri* contain a wealth of ideas and of designs, both creative and functional; they turned out to be one of the most successful public relations books in history. He was also a prolific builder, and understood thoroughly practical problems, which he explained to make his book both inspiring and useful.

Palladio took the large Italian farm, with its many scattered buildings, and unified the composition (in the process creating a hierarchy of spaces), making the organization appealing to the following generations of country gentlemen of Europe and America. He raised his one important floor, or *piano nobile*, on a high basement that became the main living space of the family, with high ceilings for coolness in the hot summers, and mezzanine rooms tucked in to upper spaces in the Roman fashion. Supporting wings to house farm services — such as, smoke houses, dairies, stables, coach houses, wash houses, etc. — were laid out on either side of the main block to frame it symmetrically. These were connected to the main house by means of colonnades or arcades and were designed as quadrants or straight hyphens, for protection in all weather. To crown it all, he often placed the hay barn on top of the main block, not only to emphasize it, but also to complete the final hierarchy of spaces and uses of areas into a single complex. Also, he integrated the house into the landscape in such a way that the total conception became the important consideration, based upon his own harmony of proportion used on all exterior parts as well as interior spaces. Above all, Palladio's durability probably rests upon his system of proportions, as expressed in his book. In any study of the principles and philosophy of architecture, the question of proportions comes up, and not the least successful of this search for a harmonic scale was formulated in *The Modulor* of Le Corbusier, published in the mid-twentieth century.

Where Palladio had been careful to relate his proportions for each space to others in a single complex, and to relate the exterior proportions to each element, and to express the plan and its functions on the exterior, the Burlingtonians in England confined themselves to a strict reading of Palladio's rules. They thus produced a rigid whole out of single units, and isolated the Palladian opening against blank walls, instead of using it as a counterpoint to the verticals and horizontals in a gallery composition, as for example, in the galleries which Palladio added to the Basilica in Vicenza.

A knowledge of Palladio's works reached the North American colonies not only through translations of the *Quattro Libri* but through the writings of such English author-architects as Colin Campbell, whose very influential *Vitruvius Britannicus* appeared in 1727, and James Gibbs, who made an adapted Palladianism popular through his *Book of Architecture*, published in 1728. Gibbs' book was widely used in America both before and after the Revolution; its influence can be seen in the designs of many buildings along the Atlantic seaboard. It should be noted, however, that American builders, using English books as patterns, picked up details of Palladio's designs rather than embracing the fundamental principles that he embodied in his works.

A brief discussion of the development of American architecture at this point may be useful. The seventeenth century is called Jacobean because it was primarily a mixture of Gothic survival plans and details with Renaissance details, whose introduction into England had formed the basis of the style there. The Parson Capen house is a notable example in New England. The Georgian style dominated the eastern seaboard from 1700 to 1776. During the first forty years, we have the Early Georgian, as seen at Drayton Hall, based on Palladio and on Wren; then High Georgian, in which the Palladian ideas, filtered through the work of Lord Burlington, Colin Campbell, and James Gibbs, became popular. Mount Airy is a beautiful plantation house with these characteristics, with flankers and colonnaded quadrants. Late Georgian lasted until after the Revolution, and consisted of buildings broken up into a series of blocks, of which Brandon in Virginia and the Hammond-Harwood house in Annapolis are notable examples. The Federal period followed, and it has been called by various

125. *Drayton Hall, 1740, on the Ashley River, South Carolina. Entrance front.*
126. *Drawing of Drayton Hall, 1740 or before.*

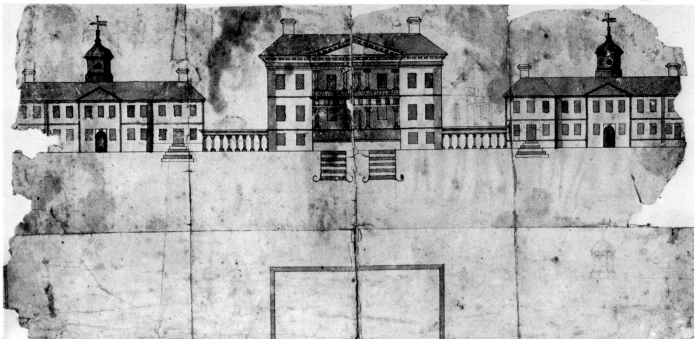

names, such as — Adamesque, Pompeian, and Neo-classical, all of which indicate derivations. Of this period, Jefferson was the outstanding voice in the demand for a fresh American architecture; freed of the restraints of the vanquished British domination, he introduced the temple form, which had been restricted in England to garden structures, and created not only a precedent for domestic architecture, but a frontispiece for all Virginia as well. Except for a single Greek garden gazebo, Jefferson preferred Roman architecture. The Greek war of independence in 1820 inspired a mania for Greek things in the United States, including a Greek Revival in architecture. When at the University of Virginia, Jefferson built his temple-form pavilions, connected with colonnades, prosperous southern planters on their way to spend the summers at Virginia springs passed through Charlottesville and saw Jefferson's pavilions with practical balconies; when they returned home they threw porticos with pediments around their plain farmhouses, as well as across the fronts. No matter that the porticos often became galleries, or outdoor living rooms, with cast-iron columns. The Greek Revival in the South had been created. Gloucester, in Natchez, is a beautiful example of a plantation house in the deep South in a rural town. The front has a handsome portico, but the garden side has a galleried porch set *in antis*, a favorite device in formal Neo-classical houses. The order is Roman Doric, and the octagonal ends betray the influence of Jefferson, although the plan is a unique development peculiar to the locality: there are two front doors, each leading into a hall with its own stair, separated by central rooms and passages. While most southern towns were rural in character, Charleston, South Carolina, was thoroughly urban. The row houses were turned at right angles to the street to provide ventilation with a garden between each house, and galleries were developed with three or more stories on the garden side to catch every breeze. Sometimes these galleries turned into Jeffersonian Roman porticos, raised on brick arches, like the lovely Guggenheim-Jenrette house on East Bay.

In 1840, a revolution in the art of architecture began. American architecture, no matter what its local characteristics, had followed one un-written rule: symmetry. Even the Jacobean structures of the first century in the New World had been symmetrical. With the advent of the Gothic Revival at this time, assymmetry, open planning, and Palladio's old dictum that exteriors should express the functions of the plan and that the landscape should fit the buildings, were principles that became the watch-word. A. J. Davis, at Lyndhurst, near Tarrytown, N.Y., and in the integration of land and buildings at Llewellyn Park, N.J., created superb essays in the taste of the times; but the final stamp of approval was set in the monumental work of two architects trained at the Beaux-Arts in Paris — Richard M. Hunt and H. H. Richardson. At mid-century, the Italianate villa and the style of the Second Empire also became favorites. In the last decades of the century the more fruitful stick and shingle styles appeared, and produced some notable houses: particularly the Stoughton house in Cambridge, and the Low house in Rhode Island. In 1893, the World's Fair in Chicago, not only fostered a splendid new park on the Chicago water-front, but also the rise of the Beaux Arts Classical Revival. The magnificent story of the invention of the skyscraper in Chicago does not concern us here. At the Breakers, in Newport, Hunt created a superb essay in the style, but also revived the Palladian motifs, along with a Bramantine gallery, on the ocean side of the house. Also in the latter part of the nineteenth century, the firm of McKim, Mead and White made a famous trip to New England and invented the Colonial Revival, so impressed were they with the Georgian and Federal buildings they found there. Both Louis Sullivan and Frank Lloyd Wright did houses in the style in their early years, and it was to come to fruition in the next century, when Palladio was rediscovered.

In the ferment just before World War I, new frontiers were created in all the arts, and the "International Style", as it was called, was born. It, and its many new directions and ramifications, need not concern us here except for one important facet of Palladianism in North America. Rarely does scholarship effect the practice of architecture, Winckelmann and Ruskin being notable exceptions. But in the mid-twentieth century a seminal study appeared: *Architectural Principles in the Age of Humanism*, by Rudolph Wittkover. This important work emphasized Palladio's system of proportions, and leading architects began to experiment with them, notably Alison and Peter Smithson at Hunstaunton School in England. Once again Palladio had fathered another revival.

Palladianism of the English variety was brought to America by Peter Harrison in the Redwood Library at Newport, Rhode Island, of 1749. The central pedimented motif, framed by the broken pediment to roof the side aisles, was a device which Palladio used in at least three of his Venetian churches, beginning with San Francesco della Vigna. It had become popular for garden temples and gazebos in England, and was literally shown in Hoppus' *Palladio*, 1735-6, and Issac Ware's *Designs from Inigo Jones and others*, 1740, both volumes of which Harrison owned. The plan is taken almost literally from Ware's book. Fiske Kimball put it very well when he wrote that "Harrison was the forerunner, as Jefferson was the founder, of American classicism". Peter Harrison was born in York, England; he was a very young man as the Earl of Burlington was erecting the famous Assembly Rooms; it is not surprising that Harrison introduced his brand of Palladianism. At King's Chapel, Boston, Harrison built with a rather heavy hand another Palladian building, and earmarks of the style are to be seen in his other buildings in New England. The Brick Market, built in 1761-2 by Harrison in Newport, has an arcade on the ground floor, and the second and third floors are unified by a colossal order. The design is taken almost literally from Old Somerset House, London, by Inigo Jones, as Downing and Sculley have pointed out. It had been published by Colin Campbell in *Vitruvius Britannicus* in 1727. Actually the design is more unified in three dimensions than the original, because it lacks the low wings which flanked that.

The first of all the houses with porticos was Whitehall, built in 1765-70 by Governor Sharpe of Maryland, with assistance by William Buckland, and it was patterned on the same kind of small garden casinos as the Redwood Library. It consisted of only one room with one-story wings, and the temple form was not to become popular until Jefferson used it for the first time in his monumental Virginia capitol.

The earliest Palladian plan was at the Orphan-house in Bethesda, Georgia. Begun in 1740, the plan was a daring and advanced design for such an early date. While early Georgian plans placed the stairs in the center hall, in the Orphan-house the Palladian arrangement of suppressing the stairs inside the halls and treating the entrance as a wide salon was adopted. This arrangement was particularly suitable to the architecture of the south where hot summers like those of the Veneto made the hall a so-called summer living room. It did not become general in southern architecture until after 1758, when it was used

127. *Redwood Library, 1749, Newport, Rhode Island. Peter Harrison, architect.*
128. *Edward Hoppus*, Palladio, *1736. Introduction to Fourth Book.*

at Mount Airy, Richmond County, Virginia. The plan of Blandfield in Essex county, Virginia, 1771, resembles that of the Orphan-house, and here the large salon opens to two stairs separating the end rooms. The arrangement of the story-and-one-half advance buildings suggests the Governor's Palace in Williamsburg, while the appearance of the house with its wide piazzas is characteristic of coastal Georgia.

Until the advent of Thomas Jefferson as an architect, Palladianism was limited in North America to the use of his Venetian windows, to the rustication in wood, which was so popular in the New World, and to the use of double porticos and to the use of plans after Palladio, with large central halls and quadrants connecting dependencies or wings. This tendency is illustrated in another of Buckland's buildings, rectangular Gunston Hall. Here a large, simple house, almost vernacular in its traditional one and one half story mass with dormers is given some distinction by the use of two diminuitive porticos. The one on the land side of the plantation house is embellished with a Palladian portico, in which a central arch is flanked by two lower rectangular openings. This device seems to have been invented by Bramante at the *Nymphaeum*. This mannerist device of Palladio, in which an arched and trabeated form of structure are combined (that is, columns and lintels used with an arch), is to be found in windows and in doorways. One reason for its popularity is that it fits neatly into a gable roof. Another is that when filled with windows and doors, it can be used successfully for entrances, or exits to balconies, where it provides an accent.

Both in the Georgian period and in the Federal period this Palladian motif was used in various ways, and with various other elements. One regional combination is found only in the Litchfield-Farmington area in Connecticut. It consists of a frontispiece used to enrich the entrance with columns below and a Palladian window above. George Washington selected a plate from Gibbs for his banquet room at Mount Vernon. The arch, with its Gibbs surround, is flanked by two angle pediments, and the pilasters are square like those on the great portico on the river front. Square columns were often used in America because they were easier to build, and that is probably the reason they were used here. A similar design without the angle pediments was used at Mount Airy, where it was expressed in stone, where it lit the stair landing, a favorite location for this motif. At Mount Pleasant, Philadelphia, it lit the upper hall, and the siting, rusticated

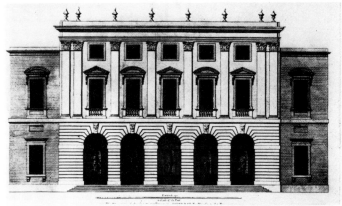

129. *Brick Market, 1761, Newport, Rhode Island. Peter Harrison, architect.*

130. *Old Somerset House, London. Inigo Jones, architect, from Colin Campbell*, Vitruvius Britannicus, *1727.*

131. *Mount Airy, 1758, Richmond County, Virginia. William Buckland, architect.*

basement, and symmetrical flankers indicate the source of its design.

The motif appeared even more regularly during the Federal era. At the first Harrison Gray Otis house, by Charles Bulfinch, Boston, it is used with the delicate attenuated columns of Adam on the second floor, and is surmounted by Palladio's thermal window on the third. At the Read house in New Castle, Delaware, it is used with a wrought iron balcony. Other examples of the Palladian motif used with thermal windows occur in the beautiful Manigault house in Charleston, and in the side elevations of the White House. At the Nightingale house in Providence the motif is used on both the entrance door, and for the window above, which has the Gibbs surround in wood over the arch. Sometimes, as at the Woodlands, Philadelphia, the entire motif would be set in a single arch, a device first used by Palladio in a very early drawing.

The Palladian plans with wide central halls, and stairs set in alcoves, are to be seen at Sabine Hall, and Mount Airy, Virginia. The Palladian complex with wings connected to the house are too numerous to mention, but some are of unusual interest. Mount Vernon has quadrants of wooden arches, Mount Airy has closed quadrants in front and open ones behind, and quadrants of columns were planned at Drayton Hall. Original uses of the Palladian court, whose arrangement is determined by integrating the house with the site are to be found at Monticello and Bremo, the former designed by Jefferson, the latter based upon his ideas. At Monticello the L-shaped wings are set ingeniously against the hill, so they will not interfere with the view; at Bremo the wings are set at right angles to the house, and are connected to it by means of colonnades on the ground level and Jeffersonian terraces above.

Two of the rare examples of drawings of Palladian plantations have only come to light in the last several years. The earliest was built in 1740, Drayton Hall on the Ashley River in South Carolina. The plan has a central block with a separate entrance hall, and a grand stair on the water side, and it had been planned to connect the large flankers with colonnades. The exteriors of the main block are particularly north Italian with the two story portico from the Villa Pisani at Montagnana, and the river front with tabernacles around the upper windows and a kind of reverse Palladian motif under the stair, that is — a rectangular entranceway framed by two lower niches. This splendid plantation is in a remarkable state

132. *Gunston Hall, 1755-1758, Fairfax County, Virginia. Entrance front. Interiors by William Buckland.*
133. *Mount Vernon, 1740, 1757-1759, 1773, before 1787. George Washington, architect for the alterations.*

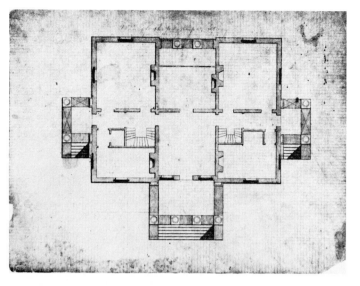

134, 135. Bremo, 1818, Fluvanna County, Virginia. John Neilson, architect, with General J.H. Cocke and Thomas Jefferson. Ink and wash drawings by Cornelia Jefferson Randolph.

of preservation, and plans are being made to preserve it carefully. The same portico is also at the Brewton House.

The other drawing, for Menokin, Virginia, may be by William Buckland, the poor boy who was apprenticed for four years to the builder of Gunston Hall. His skills as an architect were immediately recognized and before the end of his short life, his portrait was painted by Charles Willson Peale, in his hand he had a drawing of his beautiful Hammond-Harwood house in Annapolis. The drawings of Menokin show a house with un-connected flankers, a rusticated basement, and the Gibbs surround in stone framing the openings. It was built about 1769, and as Buckland had finished his work at Mount Airy in 1758, and moved to Annapolis, the rather provincial and crude details are the work of the local craftsmen.

The largest of all of these houses with flankers was Rosewell, 1725 Virginia. Destroyed by fire, it had large L-shaped flankers, and the bricks were omitted on the sides of the building where the hyphens were to be attached.

Bremo is also one of the outstanding examples of Palladio's principle of designing a building to harmonize with the landscape, and it displays one of Jefferson's favorite ideas. He liked to site a house on an eminence, so the upper portion could appear to be one story high at the entrance level, and the lower could open out at ground level. The Palladian motif here is used to enrich the ends of the outbuildings in an unusual way: rectangular plastered panels frame a single arched plastered panel. As this motif was never used by Jefferson, it probably was the suggestion of the owner, General John H. Cocke.

Since Jefferson always regarded Palladio as his master, as he told his friends who were engaged in building, it is not surprising that his philosophy of architecture parallelled that of the Venetian architect. His ideas on integrating the house and landscape, proportions of rooms and details, and the uniting of the house and its service buildings into one organized complex are all strictly Palladian. Because of the ever present danger of fire in America, where even brick buildings had floors and joists and often even studs of wood, Jefferson and the Americans never considered putting hay in their attics to build up the central block. Palladio was able to do it, because his buildings were entirely of brick tile or masonry, except for the doors, windows and rafters. Even his door and window frames were painted on plaster to simulate mouldings. On a much smaller scale, Jefferson followed the precepts of Palladio wherever possible.

To Jefferson as well as Latrobe must be given the credit for the durability of Romantic Classicism — that combination of the classical with the picturesque, which was to continue to our own day. B.H. Latrobe not only worked with and under the supervision of Jefferson, but he had high regard for the talents of the nativeborn architect, even though he preferred Roman, while Latrobe preferred Greek architecture. Latrobe really meant the orders, because some of his notable buildings contain Roman domes and masses, namely — the Baltimore Cathedral and the earlier Bank of Pennsylvania. But in order to understand the contribution of Jefferson to Palladianism and to the whole architecture in his time, we need to review briefly his career.

Tudor Place was built in 1816 by William Thornton. The exterior walls are brick, treated with plaster marked off to look like stone of a pale yellow color. This device was a favorite of Palladio's. On the garden side a circular "temple", as it is still called, opens off the central hall. There are wings connected by glass hyphens, one of which is an orangerie. The site is superb, at the crest of a hill overlooking the Potomac at Georgetown. This is one of the finest Palladian inspired houses in America.

Immediately before 1820, William Jay, an English trained architect, came to Savannah, and created his daring, yet subtle spatial concepts. At the Habersham house there is a Palladian window and the portico is similar to that at Tudor Place. The circle is also used in the free-standing stair on the interior and the entrance hall leads to a circular sitting room on the garden. At Washington, Georgia, the Alexander house has the same window used in the gable. This is an unusual detail for the south, and it is found in Connecticut, where it occurs frequently. At Hopeton there was a triple-arched loggia in the style of Palladio, built in 1830.

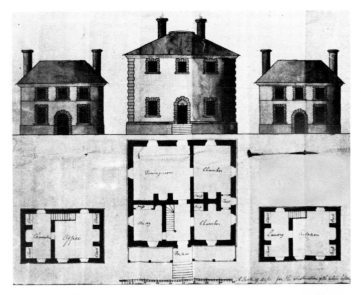

136. *Menokin, c. 1769, Richmond County, Virginia. William Buckland, architect. Water-color.*
137. *The Bank of Pennsylvania, 1799-1801, Philadelphia. B.H. Latrobe, architect. Water-color.*

138. *Tudor Place, 1816, Georgetown, D.C. Garden front.*

Thomas Jefferson during the years of his diplomatic mission to France came to know at first hand not only some Roman buildings but contemporary works of Romantic Classicism. He sketched and studied the Paris church of Sainte Genévieve (now the Pantheon), designed in 1775 by J.G. Soufflot, who had studied at the school in Rome maintained by the French state for the post-graduate training of artists. Jefferson also admired the Doric Temple at Hagley in Worcestershire, which he visited in 1788 during his tour of English gardens with John Adams. The temple had been built in 1758 by Jemas Stuart, co-author with Nicholas Revett of the great architectural work, the *Antiquities of Athens*.

Also in the 1780's, (Jefferson was there from 1784-89), Paris saw the flowering of two brilliant and original architects, L. E. Boullée and C.N. Ledoux. Both younger than Soufflot, they have been called the first great Romantic Classical architects. The eve of the French Revolution not being a propitious time for building, their work was mainly known through Ledoux's great book *L'Architecture considerée* of 1804 and through their pupils, Jefferson and N. J. Durand. Jefferson was fortunate in having the opportunity to see two early works of Boullée and Ledoux. As a close friend of the Comte and Comtesse de Tessé, he often visited their country house, Chaville, built by Boullée, and he and Maria Cosway visited Louveciennes, built for Madame du Barry. He also knew Ledoux's *barrières*, both the exciting one of St. Martin and the one built outside his window in the Champs Elysées. As these buildings were transitional, they helped to make the eager Jefferson aware of the great developments in architecture in Paris, that made it the magnet for young architects all over Europe. All of this helped to advance Jefferson's taste, and whether or not he knew the writings of these avantgarde architects, he did go out of his way to meet some of them, namely Molinos. Their works influenced greatly his own work after his return to America, and their writings would have appealed to him as they were sociological as well as architectural, and prepared him for the masterpieces of his old age.

The bold, simple masses of Romantic Classicism, the use of geometrical shapes, the interest in new material, the quest for the functional, and the impersonal and non-regional, or international character of the period from 1780-1815, have been repeated in the contemporary architecture of our own day. One may indeed call these architects the first cubists, in their insistence on the use of the sphere, pyramid, and cylinder. One thinks of the cylinder of the new Hirschorn Museum in Washington, the inverted pyramid of the new city hall in Tempe, Arizona, and the sphere of the World's Fair in New York, 1969. The sphere and the cylinder were all introduced into America by Jefferson, as we shall see.

While Romantic Classicism was primarily French in origin, the other important movement in the arts at the time was definitely English: the picturesque. Early on, it manifested itself primarily through the *jardins anglais* of the English, and the garden temples by Jefferson were primarily designed in this manner. He was particularly taken by Edmund Burke's use of the "sublime" and used it in his writings as well as his building. It was also a term used to express the glories of architecture as well as of nature. For example, Jefferson speaks of the "sublime" expression of nature to be found in the Natural Bridge of Virginia, which he purchased to prevent its exploitation.

In France, Palladianism was filtered through Gallic taste; her artists always insisted on the freedom to follow their own ideas, no matter what the fashion. Close to Italy in their cultural inclinations, the French readily felt at home with the works of Palladio, whether in public or private buildings. The beautiful Hôtel de Salm and St. Philippe de Roule, both in Paris, are characteristic of the elegance of French Palladianism, and both influenced Jefferson's own buildings. Built in 1786 by Pierre Rousseau for the rich and luxurious Prince de Salm, the former is a good example of the style. Even though the courtyard was rather conventionally Palladian, the river front with its oval niches for busts, its many glass doors, and above all the dome, was the highest expression of French Palladianism. Jefferson watched the house being built, and as it emerged from its scaffolding fell madly in love with it, as he himself said. It not only was influential in the remodelling of Monticello, but was an important design source for Farmington, Virginia. Finished in 1826, another of Jefferson's inspirations was based on St. Philippe de Roule, which Chalgrin had designed in 1772: it was Charlottesville's Christ Church, demolished in the late 19th century. Both had porticos *in antis*, panels on the upper walls flanking the portico, and the Doric order.

Jefferson knew both the transitional buildings that contained elements of the Louis XVI style and that of the *avant-garde*, or visionary style. Among the tenets of the latter was its insistence on the use of geometric forms, the sphere, cylinder, and the octagon. Jefferson

139. *Monticello, 1768-1809, Albemarle County, Virginia. Thomas Jefferson, architect. Wash and ink drawing by Robert Mills.*
140, 141. *Poplar Forest, 1806-1812, near Lynchburg, Virginia. Thomas Jefferson, architect. Ink and wash drawings by Cornelia Jefferson Randolph, c. 1820.*

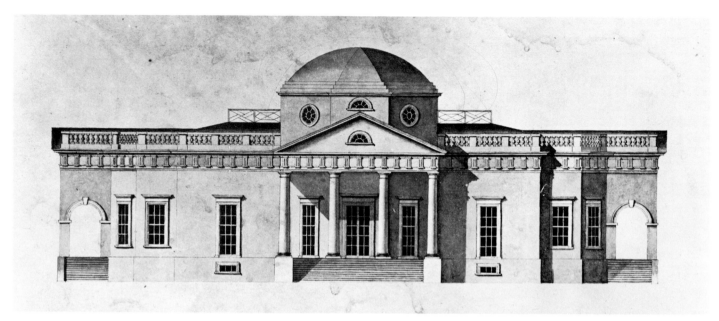

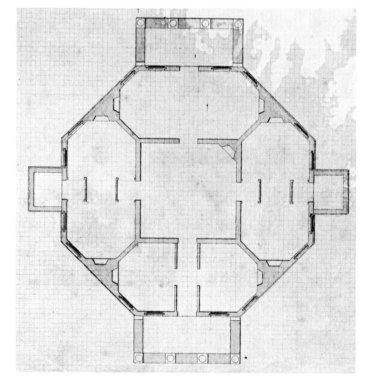

was to use all of these to perfection in his later buildings.

For his retreat at Poplar Forest, he chose the octagon, a form which dictated the exterior envelope, the shape of all of its rooms except the dining room, and even its exterior terraces. In the ceiling of the dining room is set a skylight. This motif was a favorite of Boullée, who admired overhead lighting, and used it at Chaville.

On either side of the dining room are two large octagons, in which the alcove bed is set in the middle of the room. It provides a division, or a space divider, so the bedrooms have both a dressing and sitting area — a most practical and logical arrangement.

Like most that Jefferson designed, the house is set on the edge of a rise, so that it has one story at the entrance and two at the garden side. This gives the drawing room a second portico, which is raised above the garden.

This is an eminently practical house, set in the octagonal form, but the imaginative use of space and light, and the diagonal direction of the dining room, make it a masterpiece.

But if Poplar Forest is Jefferson's domestic masterpiece it was at the University of Virginia that Jefferson was to achieve the masterpiece in a complex of buildings. With its long axis dominated by a spherical building adopted from the Pantheon, framed by a courtyard whose columns are interrupted at intervals by pavilions for the professors, this is, indeed, a masterly composition. On either side of this grand courtyard, which has been called the loveliest atrium in America, a row of student rooms with a hotel (as Jefferson called it) or commons at each end and one in the middle formed the complex to house two hundred students and ten professors. Each room was provided with cross ventilation, and a fireplace, and as far as possible, all of the schoolrooms in the individual pavilions opened to the south. All of the drawing rooms in the upper floors of the pavilions were provided with iron Franklin (or more accurately, Pennsylvania) stoves, which were economical of firewood, and radiated more heat than brick fireplaces.

The entire complex of the University of Virginia is a superb and original design, a masterpiece created from many sources of design, primarily Palladio and the visionary architects. From his books, Jefferson knew the great Villa Meledo by Palladio, where the hierarchy of the parts is emphasized by means of a series of rising terraces, or platforms. The Lawn is designed with three great terraces, building up to a rotunda like the one at Meledo. The design of the ranges is taken literally from

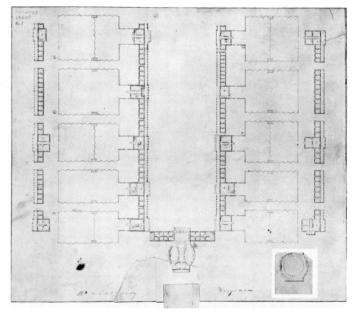

142. *The University of Virginia from the south, 1817-1826, Charlottesville. Ink and watercolor by Cornelia Jefferson Randolph, c. 1820.*

143. *Ground Plan, University of Virginia, 1817-1826, Charlottesville. Thomas Jefferson, architect. Engraving by Peter Maverick, 1824.*

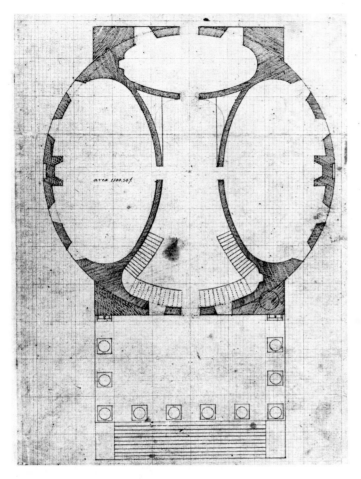

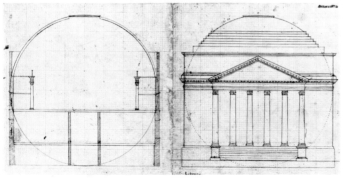

144, 145. Plan, Section and Elevation of the Rotunda, 1817-1826, University of Virginia, Charlottesville. Thomas Jefferson, architect.

the outbuildings here and at other colonnaded villas, along with the colonnades of the Lawn. The Roman Doric colonnades in the courtyard of the Hôtel de Salm also influenced the Lawn. The basic design, with a series of pavilions framing a rotunda, is similar to the Chateau de Marly, Louis XIV's favorite house near Versailles. As Jefferson said, his focal building, the Rotunda, was designed after the Pantheon in Rome at half scale. He not only used Palladio's drawings of it, but those for the restoration of the Pantheon made by Piranesi.

The Rotunda, itself, is a masterpiece of imaginative architecture. Set on a sloping site, Jefferson was able to restore the old podium and the stairs (which originally led up to the Pantheon) and thus gave it a suitable base. On the ground and first floors he designed three great oval rooms, connected by an hour-glass entrance hall, and still managed to include the Dome room under the dome. All of this is enclosed in a perfect sphere inscribed in a cylinder, a masterly solution. If we may call visionary architecture, based on geometrical forms, "cubist", then this is one of the "cubist" buildings of world architecture.

When one considers the general state of architecture in America when the Rotunda was built, one is struck by its extreme originality. For example, there is Gore Place, Waltham, Massachusetts, with its free-standing circular stair and its oval dining and living rooms, and even the White House in Washington, D.C. (and it must be remembered that Jefferson did assist in its completion) with its oval room, but these were all separate spaces which one entered without any spatial relationship to each other. Only at the Rotunda was there a successful effort to unite these spaces by means of a free-form one. It should be pointed out that this is the forerunner of the peculiarly American open, free-flowing plan, which was to be initiated by the Gothic Revival about 1840, and developed by Frank Lloyd Wright in the late 19th century and ultimately expressed in the open plan of contemporary houses of the 20th century.

In the English tradition of Colin Campbell and Lord Burlington, who built adaptations of Palladio's Villa Rotonda at Mereworth Castle and Chiswick, Thomas Jefferson tried on at least two occasions to get one built in the United States. His earlier effort was for the Governor's House in Virginia, while the other he entered (under a pseudonym) in the competition for the President's House in Washington; fortunately neither was built. In the decade following Jefferson's death, however, Charles B. Cluskey and John Pell built a Governor's House at

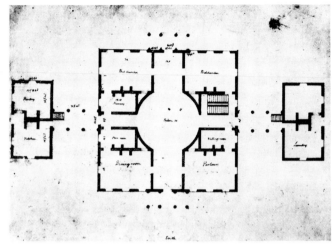

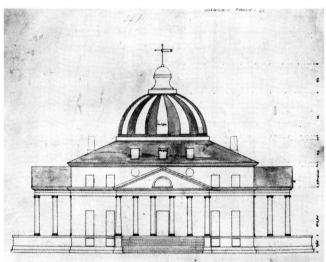

146. *Plan of the Governor's House, c. 1785, Richmond. A Rotunda house with wings connected by colonnades. Thomas Jefferson, architect.*

147. *Competition drawing for the White House, 1792, Washington. Thomas Jefferson, architect. Ink and water-color. Signed Abraham Faws.*

148. *Governor's Mansion, 1838, Milledgeville, Georgia. Charles B. Cluskey and John Pell, architects.*

149. *President's House, 1855, University of Alabama, Auburn.*

Milledgeville, Georgia, which was vaguely inspired by the Villa Rotonda. There, however, the stairs were placed off the circular domed hall on axis. There is only one Ionic portico of four columns, but on axis with it there is an octagonal drawing room.

At the President's House, University of Alabama, we see the fruition of Jefferson's use of Romantic Classicism, as well as his wish to Romanize America. The exterior is taken directly from his Pavilion V, at the University of Virginia, where Jefferson used the Ionic order of Palladio. The only change was in raising on an arcaded basement story. It was completed in 1855.

Jefferson was to be more successful than he could have dared to wish, for the semi-Palladian, Georgian, and Adamesque forms and detail continued in one form or another in American domestic architecture from 1700 right to our own day, with the exception of the period 1840-1870. The reason for the durability of the style (and even such disparate architects as A. J. Davis and Frank Lloyd Wright felt the pull of symmetry in their designs) lies partly in the stature and prestige of Jefferson, partly due to a longing for tradition and stability, due to the mobile nature of American life. The regional characteristics of Palladian-Georgian architecture do not necessarily stay regional; Maryland High Georgian is to be found on Long Island, Virginia Georgian in Texas, and Early Georgian from New England to the South, with minute versions of Mount Vernon and Monticello in almost every state.

COLONIAL REVIVAL
AND LATE PALLADIANISM

One other factor, which has contributed to the persistence of the Palladian tradition is the close ties with England which North America has always had. The medieval tradition in architecture in America has had only sporadic spurts of fashion — that is, the Gothic Revival of the nineteenth century, and the Tudor Revival and Collegiate Gothic Revival of the early twentieth century. In England it was, and still is, very strong. But the Americans have preferred their own so-called Colonial Revival, with its Palladian overtones, which has persisted down to the present day.

In 1890-1, McKim, Mead and White designed Beacon Rock at Newport. It had an excellent open plan, expressing the site on a cliff overlooking the ocean, a colonnaded courtyard framed by a pair of temple-form wings. Also in Newport is the Crossways by the same firm, built in 1898. It has a monumental portico in wood, a feature that was to become a typical motif of the Colonial Revival, which the firm invented. By the same firm, Rosecliff, 1901-02, is Louis XVI in character, but the wings are each terminated by Venetian doors. All over America for the next twenty years, Palladian motifs and porticos were used on Colonial Revival buildings.

In the hands of Hunt and Richardson, who were strong individualists, the training they had received in Paris enabled them to establish the Beaux Arts tradition. Younger men carried it on and developed it, such as — McKim, Mead and White, Carrère and Hastings, Harvey Wiley Corbett, and Charles Platt. While much of the character of this movement is French in the logic of the plans, and the monumental progression of spaces, the Palladian influence is to be seen in a renewed interest in the study of proportion, and its relationship, in the expression of the interior spaces on the exterior, and above all, in the integration of house and site. Indeed, along with the glass skyscraper, which may also be a doomed invention, the American country house developed a grace, a liveability and a sense of comfort in the first half of the twentieth century that has never been surpassed. The architects who created them include: Delano and Aldrich; Harrie Lindeberg; David Adler; Dwight James Baum; Perry, Shaw and Hepburn; John F. Staub; Neal Reid; Hentze, Adler, and Shutze; Treanor and Fatio; William Wilson Wurster; and John Russell Pope. All of these used Palladio's ideas, and Pope created the greatest Palladian buildings of the twentieth century.

A variant, via France, of the Palladian tradition, as seen in the Villa Ferretti Angeli at Dolo on the Brenta

150. The Morgan Library, 1906, New York City. Charles F. McKim, architect.

151. Faulkner Farm, c. 1913, Brookline, Massachusetts. Charles Platt, architect.

river near Venice, was used in some of the houses of the Beaux Arts tradition. Besides Rosecliff, the Frick house in New York, by Carrère and Hastings, is enriched on the façade with flat pilasters, usually in the Ionic order. A literal copy in wood was built in Hartford of the Villa Ferretti Angeli: it is the Austin house. A monumental phalanx of Doric columns and porticos graced the vanished Pennsylvania Station in New York, by McKim, Mead and White, and these were Palladian, although the interior of the station was based on the Roman baths. By the same firm, the Boston Public Library, and the New York Public Library by Carrère and Hastings have Palladian elements. One of the masterpieces in the style is the Morgan Library, New York, by McKim, Mead and White, and it is the most Palladian of them all with the Venetian motif used on the entrance porch, the whole topped by a dome.

One of the most famous of all buildings in the Beaux Arts tradition is the Pan American Union, in Washington. Paul Cret was awarded the prize in a competition for the design of it. The elevation is based upon the Villa Pisani at Bagnolo, by Palladio, with two towers framing an arched loggia. A simplified version of a one story building by the Venetian architect is to be seen in the Rodin Museum built in Philadelphia.

The art of the country house in America reached its apex in the first three decades of the twentieth century. The rise of affluence, the decline of the summer hotel, and a new semi-suburban life style which placed the emphasis on tennis and swimming instead of hunting and riding, quick transportation and the desire to use the estate for weekends during the whole year, made the new country house smaller, more practical, and with less acreage; yet treated lavishly with terraces, pools, tennis courts, and various gardening devices.

Of all the architects of this time, Charles Platt was probably the most Palladian, as his houses were often of stucco or whitepainted wood, and the Venetian motif was a favorite along with wide porticos, and classical pergolas or colonnades, tying the house to the garden.

Platt studied gardens in Italy, and wrote a book about them. He always insisted on designing the sites so that the house would be closely integrated with the land. This Palladian influence is to be seen in the Casino at Faulkner Farm, Brookline, Massachusetts, with colonnaded quadrants made into a focal point of the garden. Another similar pavilion, facing a pool, is to be found at Woodston, Mount Kisco, New York. A Palladian motif do-

118

152. Gwinn, Cleveland, Ohio, c. 1912. Charles Platt, architect.

153. Studio, c. 1920, Mrs. Harry Payne Whitney, Long Island. Delano and Aldrich, architects.

minates the entrance front as well as the gazebo, made of treillage, in the garden at Girdle Ridge, Katonah, New York. His George Maxwell Memorial Library would be at home in Vicenza, itself.

One of Charles Platt's most brilliant adaptations of the site and building is the Gwinn near Cleveland, Ohio. Here the house and garden are designed to enclose a small bay on the shores of Lake Erie. The Freer Gallery in Washington is the finest of American granite buildings of the period, with vigorous rustication and an elevation that recalls Palladio's Villa Marcello at Bertesina, near Vicenza.

David Adler of Chicago, was another important member of the group of architects who flourished before World War II. He was a reticent and retiring man, and it is said that he was the only designer in his firm. He was one of the most gifted of the group working on domestic architecture, and was particularly innovative in the use of materials. One dining room by him had pilasters whose Ionic bases and capitals were made of pewter; and circular, freestanding stairs for another house had balusters supporting the rail of crystal. He designed at least fifty houses, most of them on a Baronial scale, and the architect insisted on doing the siting, landscaping and decorating as well.

The houses with Palladian influence are among his most successful. The Jones house in Santa Barbara, California, 1916, has an entrance façade of strong Palladian derivatives. A different note is struck in the colonnade, adapted from that at S. Stefano's in Venice with Ionic capitals with fluted necks, quite un-Palladian. The Smith house, Milwaukee, 1923, has an impressive garden front on the lake, with Palladian pavilions framing a double stair that descends to the lake. The Armour house, Lake Bluff, Illinois, 1931 is one of his most formal houses, and it is based on the Hammond-Harwood house in Annapolis with quadrant connectors on the wings.

Neel Reed in Georgia was another one of the group, and his firm eventually became Hentze, Adler and Shutze, as he died young. As it has been pointed out (Grady) some of his work was based on that of Charles Platt, who was a generation earlier. One of his most Italian, and successful houses is Hills and Dales, which was influenced by Platt's Timberline, Bryn Mawr, Pennsylvania. The stucco exterior, stone trim and tile roof further accentuate the character of the design. The semi-circular portico, and the motif on the garden front as well as the window over the entrance, all indicate a debt to Palladio.

120

154. Milburne, 1933-1935, Richmond, Virginia. William Lawrence Bottomley, architect.

155. *Rose Hill, 1930-1931, Greenwood, Virginia. William Lawrence Bottomley, architect.*
156. *The Frick Collection, 1913-1915, Fifth Avenue, New York. Carrère and Hastings, architects.*

Two other houses by the firm are of great interest, Swan house and that of Mills B. Lane. The former has, on the exterior, almost more of the character of a villa of the Veneto than most of the Italianate houses in America, if the detail is not particularly Palladian. The Lane house, is principally of one story with a one story portico, and carries on the tradition in the Deep South of the single story house.

A younger man in this group was George Howe of Philadelphia. One of the most imaginative houses with a kind of Palladian motif on the garden front was his own house, High Hollow. There he used random ashlar walls of stone, with brick quoins around the openings. The superb siting along the edge of a hill, the integration of terraces with the house, and the steep roof all combine in a most successful way. The spatial concept of the highly original stair, is framed with another Palladian motif.

A different treatment of the motif is to be seen at Delano and Aldrich's elegant studio for the sculptress, Mrs. Harry Payne Whitney on Long Island. By a careful study of proportions, the architect has made the side panels narrower than usual, and the central arched space larger. This device admirably ties the windows to the entire composition. The studio is closely knit into the design of a formal garden, with flower beds and a swimming pool for diversion. This is one of the most beautiful small Palladian buildings in America.

Among other examples in the style are the Bertram Work house with an exedra central motif, taken from the Roman baths. A similar entrance door, is at the Japanese Embassy in Washington. Another house in the same style but in brick is the James Burden house with the ubiquitous five part composition and two story hyphens, planned with arches. All of these houses are carefully integrated into the landscape, planned for the delights of country living, when it was possible to have many servants, and all are by Delano and Aldrich.

One of the most successful of the architects between the two world wars was William Lawrence Bottomley, who worked generally in New York, Washington and Virginia. He described architecture as he saw it:

"In this country, since the eighteenth century, we have had a succession of loosely related and generally brief phases of design rather than a continous development. Since our fine but modest Colonial period eclecticism has flourished, underlying all, however, has been a fine classical tradition reflected in a series of state capitals, public buildings and the private houses of the conservative American class. More and more, in our national work we are developing a sequence and continuity of style...

The national style in this country is certainly a modification of the old classic style, a modification which shows English influence, Italian Renaissance features and a strong feeling of our early Colonial style."

In designing one of his earliest houses, Nordley in Richmond, Virginia, Bottomley said:

"I want to have your house perfect in style and proportion, but at the same time I would like to give it a certain romantic charm and mellowness."

The house was begun in 1923. The Palladian motifs are quite evident: the central block, flanked by quadrants connecting wings, is derived from the James Burden house by Delano and Aldrich. Both houses also have arcades on the first floor of the quadrants with circular windows above, and the Burden house was derived from Whitehall, near Annapolis. The latter has recently been restored, and the upper story with the circular windows has been removed, since this was added in the late eighteenth century.

Also in Richmond, Milburne is another variant on this theme. In this very handsome design, a large central block is presented in the front, but the Palladian plan is revealed on the river front, where the end pavilions are attached by hyphens in the form of loggias.

At Rose Hill, Greenwood, Virginia, the same plan is used, but a Palladian motif has been used for the porch in the central block, as the focal point of the design. This house, like the others, has a handsome entrance court with details drawn from Gibbs' *Book of Architecture*, and the entrance doorway is derived directly from Sabine Hall, near Warsaw, Virginia. It was built in 1930-31.

The Broad Street Station, Richmond, Virginia, by John Russell Pope, is one of the most graceful of all Palladian buildings in America: it has a dome set on a drum, and in turn is set on a square, lighted with four great thermal windows. The portico has the wide spacings between the center columns to express the entrance, a detail so popular with Palladio. And it ends with terminal bays made up of arches with a mezzanine window above; the whole is surmounted with a splendid parapet, enriched with carving, a clock, and lettering. The low, symmetrical wings complete the Palladian plan.

However, the greatest Palladian building in America, in the twentieth century is the National Gallery of Art in Washington, also by Pope. Again, a marble dome with a pedimented portico on the Mall is approached

157. *Broad Street Station, 1919, Richmond, Virginia. John Russel Pope, architect.*
158. *Broad Street Station, 1919, Richmond, Virginia. Interior. John Russell Pope, architect.*

with a monumental flight of stairs, in Palladio's usual way, with terraces and walls to mask services, tying the building to the site in a skillful manner. The exterior admirably fits the plan with a great rotunda within the center, galleries behind the wings, and garden courts in the terminal pavilions. On the interior, the rotunda is finished with a peristyle of *antique verte* columns and a coffered ceiling, and there is a fountain in the center. There are also fountains in the courts, which are surrounded by peristyles of stone columns. The stairs are relegated to side halls. When one remembers that the original design had smaller porticos at the sides of the terminal pavilions, making four in all, it can be seen that Palladio's influence is to be seen everywhere in the building. For a building to house the nation's art treasures it would be hard to conceive of a more monumental and graceful structure, with that tradition which, for better or worse, has dominated American architecture for the last two hundred and fifty years.

160. National Gallery of Art, 1937-1941, Washington. Exterior view. John Russell Pope, architect.

BIBLIOGRAPHY

General works

Alabama Chapter, National League of American Pen Women, *Historic Homes of Alabama and Their Traditions*, Birmingham, 1935.

Andrews Wayne, *Architecture in New York*, New York, 1969.

Architects Emergency Committee, *Great Georgian Houses of America*, Vols. I & II, New York, 1933.

Beirce R.R. and Scarff J.H., *William Buckland*, Annapolis, 1958.

Bridenbaugh Carl, *Peter Harrison*, Chapel Hill, 1949.

Downing A.F. and Scully V.J., *The Architectural Heritage of Newport, Rhode Island*, New York, 1967.

Grady James, *The Architecture of Neel Reid in Georgia*, Athens, 1973.

Guinness and Sadler, *Mr. Jefferson, Architect*, New York, 1973.

Hamlin Talbot, *Benjamin Henry Latrobe*, New York, 1955.

Heyer Paul, *Architects on Architecture: New Directions in America*, New York, 1966.

Hitchcock H.R., *Rhode Island Architecture*, New York, 1968.

Hood Davyd F., *William Lawrence Bottomley in Virginia: The "Neo-Georgian" Houses in Richmond*, Master's Thesis, UVA, 1975.

Johnston F.B. and Waterman T.T., *The Early Architecture of North Carolina*, Chapel Hill, 1947.

A Monograph of the Works of McKim, Mead & White, 1879-1915, Vols. I-III, New York, 1915.

Nichols Frederick D., *The Early Architecture of Georgia*, Chapel Hill, 1957.

Nichols F.D. and O'Neal W.B., *Architecture in Virginia 1776-1958: The Old Dominion's 12 Best Buildings*, Richmond, 1958.

A Monograph of the Work of Charles A. Platt, New York, 1925.

Peter Armistead, *Tudor Place*, New York, 1970.

Pratt Dorothy & Richard, *A Guide to Early American Homes, North & South*, New York, 1956.

Pratt Richard, *David Adler*, New York, 1970.

Price Chester B., *Portraits of Ten Country Houses Designed by Delano & Aldrich*, New York, 1924.

Price Matlack, *The Work of Dwight James Baum, Architect*, New York, 1927.

Scully Vincent, *American Architecture and Urbanism*, New York, 1973.

Stern Robert, *New Directions in American Architecture*, New York, 1974.

Stuchbury Howard E., *The Architecture of Colin Campbell*, Manchester, 1967.

Wallace P.B., *Colonial Houses: Philadelphia*, New York, 1931.

Whiffen Marcus, *The Eighteenth Century Houses of Williamsburg*, New York & Williamsburg, 1960.

Periodicals

Bottomley William L., "A Selection from the Works of Delano & Aldrich", *The Architectural Record*, Vol. 54, No. 1, July 1923, pp. 3-71.

Childs Marquis W., "Mr. Pope's Memorial", *The Magazine of Art*, Vol. 30, April 1937, pp. 26, 202.

Davidson Marshall B., "Notable American Houses: going by the book in designs and practices", *Antiques*, Vol. 100, October 1971, pp. 580-5.

Hewlings Richard, "Palladianalysis" *The Architectural Review*, Vol. 157, February 1975, p. 114.

Kelsey and Cret, "The Pan American Union & Annex", *The Architectural Record*, Vol. 34, 1913.

"Menokin", *An Occasional Bulletin of The Virginia Historical Society*, No. 21, October 1970.

"The Restoration of Colonial Williamsburg", reprinted from the December 1935 issue of *The Architectural Record*, New York, 1935.

Wertz Sylvia S., "What and Why the Palladian Window?" *Antiques*, Vol. 27, June 1935, pp. 210-19.

PHOTOGRAPHIC CREDITS

B. Adorni, Parma: 116.

Alderman Library, University of Virginia: 127, 129, 134, 135, 142, 143, 144, 145, 146.

Architecture of McKim, Mead and White: 150.

Architecture of Charles Platt: 151.

Peter Armistead: 138.

Diego Birelli, Mestre: 7, 8, 11, 15, 16, 20, 25, 26, 27, 28, 29, 43, 47, 50, 53, 54, 59, 73, 80, 86, 90, 95, 97, 103, 106, 110, 114, 117.

Borluì, Venice: 56, 68.

Centro Internazionale Studi di Architettura « A. Palladio », 1, 3, 10, 13, 17, 18, 19, 48, 57, 66, 70, 71, 77, 81, 83, 85, 92, 101, 104, 107, 113, 124.

Cinecolorfoto, Vicenza: 21, 22.

Courtauld Institute of Art, London: 67.

Delano & Aldrich, *Ten Country Houses*: 153.

Hugh Doran, Dublin: 121.

Downing & Scully, *Architecture Heritage of Newport*: 130.

Electa Editrice, Milan: 2, 6, 14, 24, 30, 37, 42, 46, 55, 58, 60, 61, 63, 74, 76, 78, 88, 91, 94, 96, 100, 115, 119, 123.

Ferrini, Vicenza: 69.

Fiske Kimball Library, University of Virginia: 128.

Fondazione Giorgio Cini, Venice: 118.

Fototecnica, Vicenza: 4, 38, 62, 64, 65, 75, 84, 99.

The Frick Collection, New York: 156.

Historic Charleston, Inc.: 125, 126.

Library of Congress, Washington: 131, 132, 133.

Maryland Historical Society: 137, 147.

Massachusetts Historical Society: 139, 140, 141.

Museo Civico, Vicenza: 23.

National Gallery of Art, Washington: 159, 160.

F.D. Nichols, *The Early Architecture of Georgia*: 148.

Old Homes in Alabama: 149.

Mrs. Walter Robertson: 154.

A. Rossi, Venice: 9, 31, 32, 33, 36, 44, 45, 49, 79, 93, 108, 109, 111, 112, 122.

S.E.T.A.F., Vicenza: 39.

Soprintendenza ai Monumenti, Venice: 105, 120.

Tapparo e Trentin, Vicenza: 40, 41.

Vajenti, Vicenza: 5, 12, 34, 35, 52, 72, 82, 87, 98.

Virginia Historical Society: 136.

Virginia Museum of Fine Arts: 155, 157, 158.

CONTENTS